What's

That

From?

What's

The Ultimate Quiz

That

Book of Contemporary

From?

Movie Lines

JAI NANDA

St. Martin's Griffin
New York

Library of Congress Cataloging-in-Publication Data

Nanda, Jai.
    What's that from?: the ultimate quiz book of contemporary movie
  lines / Jai Nanda. —1st ed.
        p.   cm.
      ISBN 0–312–14145–9
      1. Motion pictures—Quotations, maxims, etc. I. Title.
PN1994.9.N36 1996
791.43—dc20   95–25629

Design by Bonni Leon-Berman

10 9 8 7 6 5 4

To Raj, Helena, and Alexander

"When Alexander saw the breadth of his domain,
he wept, for there were no more worlds to conquer."
—Hans Gruber,
from *Die Hard*

Contents

Acknowledgments

This book was a joint effort in many ways, and I would like to thank those responsible for its completion. Sheryl B. Fullerton, Gregg Pasternack for his contribution, Doug and Josh Schaer, Ken Rath, Jonathan Isaacs, Laurence Blum, Paul McCann, Eric Hirshhorn for his diving catch, Inter-Video Electronics (New York, New York), and my family. These thanks hereby absolve me from giving the preceding free copies.

Introduction

Many is the time I have sat around with friends quoting movies, and I noticed that we all seemed to know the same films. We don't toss around quips from *Citizen Kane* or *Gone with the Wind*, and no one tries to come up with James Cagney's five best lines. We are members of that infamous Generation X, and we quote Chevy Chase and Bill Murray. Mel Brooks and Monty Python are our Cecil B. DeMille and John Huston.

I am not, in any way, taking anything away from the "old days." I love Humphrey Bogart and Cary Grant as much as most, and there will never be others like them. But the truth is, I am not fascinated with them. And from what I can tell, neither is this generation of movie quoters.

Maybe we are a simple people, but we know what we like. Like generations before us, the movie lines we cherish have become part of our language. We use them to express our thoughts and to make us laugh. Unlike our predecessors, though, I believe more members of this generation are fluent in movie dialogue than ever before. With the advent of the VCR and the movie rental business, we are able to scrutinize movies in a way previous generations never could. We rent them again and again, or even make them a part of our permanent collection (usually by taping them off cable). One result has been a burgeoning fascination with movie lines. In greater numbers, they are being memorized, repeated, and savored; they are delicate treats revealed after multiple viewings of a film.

The majority of the films in this book are from the 1970s and '80s, although there are a few selections from the decades on either side. I have attempted to be as inclusive as possible, but the subject matter is vast and I realize there are quote buffs out there who will question my selection. Please be understanding and forgiving.

At the very least, I hope that after reading and studying this book, never again during a club function, a night out, or even a frat party, will you be forced to ask the embarrassing question, "What's that from?"

How It Works: A Reader's Guide to What's That From?

What's That From? tests general knowledge of movie trivia, but concentrates mainly on movie quotes. The book is divided into six parts. Parts I, III, and V are a quoter's paradise. Each part is a random selection of classic quotes ranging in difficulty from beginner to advanced. For each quote, identify the movie it comes from, then check your answer. Each answer is followed by a bonus question—either a trivia question about the movie or another quote. If the bonus question is a quote, your answer should be the next line of dialogue in the film. For example, if a bonus question from *Fletch* reads, "How gray?," the answer is Fletch's actual response to this question, which is "Charcoal."

Part II features groups of questions from especially quotable and popular movies. Part IV focuses on lines from some of Hollywood's most prolific actors. Part VI is a collection of quotes from specific types of movies, from Westerns to Oscar winners.

What's That From? is designed to challenge, inform, and entertain. It was written as the ultimate tribute to the great movie quotes of my generation, so the best advice I can give is when in doubt, quote! Best of luck, and enjoy the tour.

Part One

A QUOTER'S
Paradise for
Beginners

The following quotes are tossed around
enough that even if you haven't seen the
films they are from, you should be able to
recognize and identify them.

1. "Does this proposition entail my dressing up as Little Bo Peep?"

2. "Excuse me while I whip this out."

3. "I'll have what she's having."

4. "Seeing how the VP is such a VIP, shouldn't we keep the PC on the QT?"

5. "You talkin' to me? You talkin' to me? Well I'm the only one here."

6. "It's good to be the king."

7. "I think this place is restricted, Wang, so don't tell 'em you're Jewish."

8. "Anyone know what this is? Class? Anyone? Anyone?"

9. "I'll meet you at the place near the thing where we went that time."

10. "Every time I start talking about boxing, a white guy gotta pull Rocky Marciano outta his ass."

11. "When eight hundred years old you reach, look as good, you will not."

12. "Hey, babe, I negotiate million-dollar deals for breakfast, I think I can handle this Eurotrash. Hey! Sprekin' ze talk?"

1. Fletch
   How old is Grease?

2. Blazing Saddles
   "Is it true what they say about the way you people are gifted?"

3. When Harry Met Sally . . .
   Whose real-life mother says this line?

4. Good Morning, Vietnam
   What real-life disc jockey does Robin Williams play?

5. Taxi Driver
   What is the name of the political candidate that Travis (Robert De Niro) wants to kill?

6. History of the World Part One
   What character does director Mel Brooks play in the Spanish Inquisition scene?

7. Caddyshack
   What is the name of the boat owned by Judge Smails (Ted Knight)?

8. Ferris Bueller's Day Off
   In what city does the movie take place?

9. Broadcast News
   What actor plays Jack Rorsch, the New York anchorman?

10. Coming to America
    What two other characters from a previous Eddie Murphy film make a cameo in this movie?

11. Return of the Jedi
    Where do the Ewoks live?

12. Die Hard
    What is McClane's limo driver's name?

ANSWERS TO BONUS QUESTIONS

1. nineteen
2. "It's true, it's true."
3. director Rob Reiner's mother, Estelle
4. Adrian Cronauer
5. Senator Charles Palentine
6. the Grand Inquisitor Torquemada
7. *The Flying Wasp*
8. Chicago
9. Jack Nicholson
10. Randolph and Mortimer Duke (Don Ameche and Walter Bellamy) from *Trading Places*
11. the Planet Moon of Endor
12. Argyle

13. "If you build it, he will come."

14. "Relax . . . My old man is a television repairman. He's got this ultimate set of tools. I can fix it."

15. "Over Macho Grande?"
"No, I don't think I'll ever get over Macho Grande. Those wounds run pretty deep."

16. "It's an eighty-eight magnum."
"It shoots through schools."

17. "Shall we play a game?"

18. "Greed, for lack of a better word, is good."

19. "Sometimes shit happens, someone has to deal with it, and who ya gonna call?"

20. "What I want out of each and every one of you is a hard target search of every gas station, residence, warehouse, farmhouse, henhouse, out-house, and doghouse in that area."

21. "He slimed me."

22. "What we've got here is a failure to communicate."

23. *"Hasta la vista,* baby."

13. Field of Dreams
    Besides this phrase, what other messages does the voice tell Ray (Kevin Costner)?

14. Fast Times at Ridgemont High
    What are the three laws posted on the wall of the All-American Burger restaurant?

15. Airplane II: The Sequel
    "Doctor, can you give the court your impression of Mr. Striker?"

16. Johnny Dangerously
    How did Danny Vermin (Joe Piscopo) fulfill a lot of people's predictions?

17. War Games
    What game does David (Matthew Broderick) choose to play?

18. Wall Street
    What character does Michael Douglas play?

19. Ghostbusters II
    Dr. Venkman (Bill Murray) is the host of what cable TV show?

20. The Fugitive
    What is the fugitive's name?

21. Ghostbusters
    When the Ghostbusters appear on *The Joe Franklin Show,* what question does he ask them?

22. Cool Hand Luke
    What happens to anyone who breaks the prison rules?

23. Terminator 2: Judgement Day
    What is the model number of this Terminator?

ANSWERS TO BONUS QUESTIONS

13. "Ease his pain" and "Go the distance."
14. "No shirt. No shoes. No dice."
15. "I'm sorry, I don't do impressions, my training is in psychiatry."
16. He became "a real scumbag."
17. Global Thermonuclear War
18. Wall Street magnate Gordon Gekko, known to his close friends as GG
19. *The World of the Psychic*
20. Dr. Richard Kimball
21. "How is Elvis, and have you seen him lately?"
22. He spends the night "in the box" (solitary confinement).
23. T-1000

24. "Didn't I tell you that the phone in my limo is busted and I can't get in contact with my bitches?"

25. "You've got me? Who's got you?"

26. "Do I make myself clear, Jerome?"
"Ho yes."
"Ho what?"
"Ho nothing . . . No ho. I mean no ho Sergeant. Just plain ho."

27. "How much for the women? Your women, I want to buy your women."

28. "Six thousand dollars? It's not even leather."

29. "Did you say 'utes'?"
"Yeah, the two utes."

30. "You're outta order. You're outta order. This whole trial is outta order."

31. "There's a new sheriff in town. And his name is Reggie Hammond. Y'all be cool. Right on."

32. "You got to ask yourself one question: 'Do I feel lucky?' Well? Do ya, punk?"

33. "This is Chevalier, Montage, Detente, Avant Garde, and Deja Vous."
"Have we met before?"

34. "Would you give me a hand with the bags?"
"Certainly. You take the blonde, and I'll take the one in the turban."

35. "But I was there . . . while pussies like you were back here partyin', puttin' on headbands, doin' drugs and listenin' to goddamn Beatle albums."

24. Trading Places
How much money do the Dukes (Ralph Bellamy and Don Ameche) place on their bet?

25. Superman
What is Superman's father's name, and what actor plays him?

26. Biloxi Blues
This movie is based on the second play in a trilogy by Neil Simon. What are the first and third plays?

27. The Blues Brothers
How long was Jake (John Belushi) in jail?

28. Working Girl
Where do Tess (Melanie Griffith) and Cynthia (Joan Cusack) live?

29. My Cousin Vinny
Which actor plays the judge?

30. . . . And Justice for All
Which actor plays Judge Fleming?

31. 48 Hours
How long has Reggie (Eddie Murphy) been in prison?

32. Dirty Harry
What type of gun is Harry (Clint Eastwood) carrying?

33. Top Secret
What does the name "Hillary" mean in Hillary's (Lucy Gutteridge) native language?

34. Young Frankenstein
Whose brain was Igor (Marty Feldman) supposed to get?

35. Back to School
What line follows Thorton Mellon's (Rodney Dangerfield) question, "What's a bath without bubbles?"

ANSWERS TO BONUS QUESTIONS

24. one dollar
25. Jar-El, played by Marlon Brando
26. *Brighton Beach Memoirs* and *Broadway Bound*
27. He served three years out of five, with time off for good behavior.
28. Staten Island, New York
29. Fred Gwynne

30. John Forsythe
31. three years
32. a .44 magnum
33. "she whose bosoms defy gravity"
34. the brain of Hans Delbruk, saint and scientist
35. "Hey Bubbles, come over here, will ya?"

36. "You fell victim to one of the classic blunders. The most famous is never get involved in a land war in Asia."

37. "Just when I thought I was out, they pull me back in."

38. "Fat, drunk, and stupid is no way to go through life, son."

39. "I don't know why they call this stuff Hamburger Helper, it does just fine by itself."

40. "No more yanky my wanky. The Donger needs food."

41. "You guys know so much about women, how come you're here at, like, the Gas 'n' Zip on a Saturday night completely alone, drinking beers, no women anywhere?"
"By choice, man, conscious choice."

42. "If I were the man I was five years ago, I'd take a flame thrower to this place."

43. "Show me 'Paint the Fence.' "

44. "Juuusssst a bit outside—tried the corner and missed."

45. "Kids. Big Ben, Parliament."

46. "Come on, sporto, level with me. Do you slip her the hot beef injection?"

36. The Princess Bride
    Who played Fezzik the Giant?

37. The Godfather Part III
    True or false: This was the only one of the three *Godfather* movies that did not win the Oscar for Best Picture?

38. National Lampoon's Animal House
    What does Blutarski (John Belushi) imitate in the cafeteria?

39. National Lampoon's Vacation
    What actor plays the Wally World security guard the Griswalds take hostage?

40. Sixteen Candles
    What item is the Geek (Anthony Michael Hall) required to show as proof that he scored with Samantha (Molly Ringwald)?

41. Say Anything . . .
    What "sport of the future" does Lloyd Dobler (John Cusak) play?

42. Scent of a Woman
    What hotel do Charlie (Chris O'Donnell) and Lieutenant Colonel Slade (Al Pacino) stay in while visiting New York?

43. The Karate Kid
    What is the name of the evil dojo?

44. Major League
    What is the name of Pedro's voodoo god?

45. National Lampoon's European Vacation
    The Griswalds win their trip on what game show?

46. The Breakfast Club
    How does Brian (Anthony Michael Hall) respond when the teacher says, "I was just in my office and I heard a ruckus"?

ANSWERS TO BONUS QUESTIONS

36. Andre the Giant
37. true
38. a zit
39. John Candy
40. "Underpants . . . Girl's underpants."
41. kickboxing
42. the Waldorf-Astoria
43. Cobra Kai
44. Jobu
45. *Pig in a Poke*
46. "Could you describe the ruckus, sir?"

47. "Hey fellas, it's on me—Shakespeare for everybody, okay? You too honey, ooh, I'd like to tame your shrew."

48. "I ate his liver with some fava beans and a nice Chianti."

49. "I love the smell of napalm in the morning."

50. "We'll do it for Johnny, man. Let's do it for Johnny."

51. "Time of your life, Joel."

52. "You just go back to your beer, Buttercrud."

53. "Come out to the coast, we'll get together, have a few laughs."

54. "No, you did not have great sex with Sheldon. . . . A Sheldon can do your income tax. If you need a root canal, Sheldon's your man."

55. "Hide me Eddie, puhleeeeease."

56. "Nah, that's not a knife. Now *that's* a knife."

57. "I'm your number-one fan."

47. Back to School
    Mellon (Rodney Dangerfield) has pictures of his wife with another man, but one of the photos is confusing. Why?

48. Silence of the Lambs
    What is Hannibal Lecter's nickname?

49. Apocalypse Now
    Which actor plays Kurtz?

50. The Outsiders
    What happened to Johnny (Ralph Maccio)?

51. Risky Business
    What is the name of the first call "girl" to show up at Joel's house?

52. The Bad News Bears
    What does Buttermaker (Walter Matthau) do for a living, besides manage Little League?

53. Die Hard
    At the end of this movie, Hans (Alan Rickman) tells McClane (Bruce Willis) that "this time John Wayne does not ride off into the sunset with Grace Kelly." What movie is he referring to?

54. When Harry Met Sally . . .
    What phrase is Sally (Meg Ryan) trying to draw during the Pictionary game?

55. Who Framed Roger Rabbit
    What actor plays Eddie, the private eye?

56. Crocodile Dundee
    Where in Australia is Dundee (Paul Hogan) from?

57. Misery
    Of what author is Annie (Kathy Bates) the number-one fan?

ANSWERS TO BONUS QUESTIONS

47. "This one I can't figure out. There's you, there's Georgio, what's with the midget?"
48. Hannibal the Cannibal
49. Marlon Brando
50. He was burned in a fire.
51. Jackie
52. He cleans pools.
53. *High Noon*
54. "baby talk"
55. Bob Hoskins
56. Walkabout Creek
57. Paul Sheldon

58. "Go ahead, make my day."

59. "You will never find a more wretched hive of scum and villainy."

60. "You want answers?"
"I want the truth."
"You can't handle the truth."

61. "I never heard of no one so shit-all stupid as you drivin' off that road. You must got manure for you brains."

62. "I cast you out, unclean spirit."

63. "I've been thinking about this, Mr. Hand. If I'm here and you're here, doesn't that make it our time?"

64. "A man becomes preeminent, he is expected to have enthusiasms."

65. "Sometimes I sing and dance around the house in my underwear, doesn't make me Madonna. Never will."

66. "It's K-K-Ken c-c-coming to k-k-kill me."

67. "Nazis. I hate these guys."

58. Sudden Impact
What makes Harry (Clint Eastwood) go back into the coffee shop and thereby disrupt the holdup?

59. Star Wars
What color and number is Luke (Mark Hamill) assigned in the battle against the Death Star?

60. A Few Good Men
Name the two characters on trial.

61. National Lampoon's Vacation
After Clark (Chevy Chase) jumps the Family Truckster off the end of the closed road, Rusty (Anthony Michael Hall) exclaims, "You must have jumped this thing about fifty yards." How does Clark respond?

62. The Exorcist
Who wrote the best-selling novel of the same name, as well as the Oscar-winning screenplay?

63. Fast Times at Ridgemont High
What three now-famous actors made their debuts in this movie—two as Spicoli's surf buddies, and one as a fry cook?

64. The Untouchables
What agency does Ness (Kevin Costner) work for?

65. Working Girl
What three things does Cynthia (Joan Cusack) offer Jack (Harrison Ford) when she lets him into Tess's (Melanie Griffith) office?

66. A Fish Called Wanda
Ken (Michael Palin) does kill Otto (Kevin Kline). How?

67. Indiana Jones and the Last Crusade
Which actor plays the young Indiana Jones?

ANSWERS TO BONUS QUESTIONS

58. There is too much sugar in his coffee.
59. Red 5
60. Lowden Downey and Harold Dawkins
61. "Nothing to be proud of, Russ . . . fifty yards."
62. William Peter Blatty
63. Anthony Edwards, Eric Stoltz, and Nico-
las Cage (using his real name in the credits, Nicolas Coppola)
64. The U.S. Treasury Department
65. "Coffee, tea, me?"
66. He runs him over with a steam roller.
67. River Phoenix

68. "The real excitement is . . . during sexual awareness week. We import two hundred hookers from around the world and each camper, armed only with a thermos of coffee and two thousand dollars cash, tries to visit as many countries as he can."

69. "Do you mind if we dance with yo dates?"

70. "It's just a flesh wound."

71. "I want my two dollars."

72. "I am not an animal, I am a human being."

73. "We did not land on Plymouth Rock, Plymouth Rock landed on us."

74. "Snakes. Why did it have to be snakes?"

75. "Let's have a bachelor party with chicks, and guns, and fire trucks, and hookers, and drugs, and booze."

76. "Go ahead. Make my millennium."

77. "I must break you."

78. "This means something. This is important."

79. "Is it safe?"

68. Meatballs
What does the winning camper get?

69. National Lampoon's Animal House
Who does Otter (Tim Matheson) say beat him up in the hotel room?

70. Monty Python and the Holy Grail
Which knight has a singing minstrel following him?

71. Better Off Dead
What is the name of the dangerous ski run?

72. The Elephant Man
What is the Elephant Man's real name?

73. Malcolm X
In the film, who is the leader of the Nation of Islam?

74. Raiders of the Lost Ark
True or false: This is the first of the Indiana Jones trilogy, but it actually is set after the sequel, *Indiana Jones and The Temple of Doom?*

75. Bachelor Party
Who is Rick (Tom Hanks) thinking of adopting?

76. Beetlejuice
What two actors play the recently deceased couple?

77. Rocky IV
Who is Rocky's (Sylvester Stallone) opponent in this one?

78. Close Encounters of the Third Kind
What is the name of the mountain where the spaceship lands?

79. Marathon Man
When Zell (Laurence Olivier) continually asks Creepy (Dustin Hoffman) "Is it safe?," what is he referring to?

ANSWERS TO BONUS QUESTIONS

68. "The winner, of course, is named King of Sexual Awareness Week and is allowed to rape and pillage the neighboring towns."
69. "It was Greggy and Douggy, and some of the other Hitler youth."
70. the Brave Sir Robin
71. the K-12
72. John Merrick
73. the Honorable Elijah Muhammad
74. True. *Raiders* opens in 1936, the sequel in 1935.
75. "I'd like to adopt this seventeen-year-old Korean girl I've had my eye on for a while."
76. Alec Baldwin and Geena Davis
77. Ivan Drago (Dolph Lundgren)
78. Devil's Top Mountain
79. He is asking if it is safe to go collect his diamonds from the jewelry store.

80. "He has a chair in history at Princeton. Oh, and the short man is Herschel Kominsky. He has a chair in philosophy at Cornell."
"Yeah. Two more chairs they got a dining room set."

81. "No, try not. Do or do not. There is no try."

82. "That's all we need, a Druish Princess."
"Funny. She doesn't look Druish."

83. "Will the dancing Hitlers please wait in the wings, we are only seeing singing Hitlers."

84. "I'm your huckleberry."

85. "Looks like I picked the wrong week to stop sniffing glue."

86. "Mrs. Robinson, you're trying to seduce me."

87. "Reap the whirlwind, Sheriff Brady. Reap it."

88. "Suppose I were to offer you one million dollars for one night with your wife."

89. "I don't want to buy anything, sell anything, or process anything as a career."

90. "I got a trig midterm tomorrow and I'm being chased by Guido the Killer Pimp."

80. Annie Hall
    True or false: Diane Keaton won the Best Actress Oscar for her performance?

81. The Empire Strikes Back
    What actor plays Lando Calrissian?

82. Spaceballs
    What actress plays the Druish Princess?

83. The Producers
    Once the play is a hit, what do Leo (Gene Wilder) and Max (Zero Mostel) try to do to ruin it?

84. Tombstone
    How does Doc Holiday (Val Kilmer) respond when asked if he's retired?

85. Airplane!
    Who plays the copilot Roger Murdock?

86. The Graduate
    What actress plays Mrs. Robinson?

87. Young Guns
    What word was chiseled into the headstone of Billy the Kid (Emilio Estevez)?

88. Indecent Proposal
    What does Diana (Demi Moore) say when Jack (Robert Redford) tells her she might actually enjoy their night together?

89. Say Anything . . .
    Which actress plays the "brain trapped in the body of a game show hostess"?

90. Risky Business
    What kind of car does Joel's (Tom Cruise) father have?

ANSWERS TO BONUS QUESTIONS

80. True. She won the award in 1977.
81. Billy Dee Williams
82. Daphne Zuniga
83. They try to blow up the theater.
84. "Not me. I'm in my prime."
85. Kareem Abdul-Jabbar
86. Anne Bancroft
87. "Pals"
88. "Don't bet on it."
89. Ione Skye
90. He has a Porsche.

Part Two

Classic Movies

The Princess Bride

1. After Vizzini says "inconceivable" for the third time, what does Inigo Montoya (Mandy Patankin) say?

2. Why does Westley (Cary Elwes) say he will let Prince Humperdinck (Chris Sarandon) keep his ears in their concluding "Fight to the Pain"?

3. What are the three terrors of the fire swamp?

4. Miracle Max (Billy Crystal) claims that true love is the best thing in the world, except for one thing. What is it?

5. Which actor plays the storyteller?

Airplane

1. Where was Ted Striker's (Robert Hays) last dogfight?

2. Who is pinch-hitting for Pedro Borbon?

3. "Surely you can't be serious?"

4. "What kind of plane is it?"

5. Which dinner was poisoned, the fish or the chicken?

The Princess Bride

1. "You keep using that word. I don't think it means what you think it means."

2. "So that every shriek of every child at seeing your hideousness will be yours to cherish."

3. The Lightning Sand, The Flame Spurts, and The ROUS (Rodents Of Unusual Size)

4. "Except for a nice MLT, mutton, lettuce and tomato sandwich . . . where the mutton is nice and lean, and the tomato's ripe."

5. Peter Falk

Airplane

1. over Macho Grande

2. Manny Mota

3. "I am serious. And don't call me Shirley."

4. "Oh, it's a big pretty, white plane with red stripes, curtains in the windows, and wheels, and it looks like a big Tylenol."

5. the fish

Hollywood Shuffle

1. What is the name of the fast food chain that Bobby Taylor (Robert Townsend) works in?

2. What review do the movie critics give *Dirty Larry?*

3. What movie do the critics give "the serious high five?"

4. What new food is the manager of Winky Dinky Dog inventing and why?

5. When is the one time a person can say "drugs" around Mr. Batty?

Die Hard

1. What are the names of the two FBI agents who are brought in to handle the situation at the Nakatomi Plaza?

2. The first time McClane (Bruce Willis) tries to radio for help, the police operator tells him that the channel he is using is for emergency use only. What does he say to her?

3. What is the "miracle" that opens the vault?

4. On the helicopter ride to the roof of the Nakatomi building, one agent tells the other that it's "just like fuckin' Saigon, hey, slick?" How does the other agent respond?

5. Name the actor who plays Hans Gruber.

Hollywood Shuffle

1. Winky Dinky Dog

2. "We give *Dirty Larry* the finger!"

3. *Attack of the Killer Pimps*

4. "Winky Dinky 'Ho Cakes. 'Ho's gotta eat, too."

5. You can say "drugs" only if you've got some.

Die Hard

1. Agent Johnson and Special Agent Johnson

2. "No fuckin' shit lady, do I sound like I'm orderin' a pizza?"

3. the FBI

4. "I was in junior high, dickhead."

5. Alan Rickman

Fletch

1. What three things does Fletch (Chevy Chase) ask for when he wakes up in the Records Room?

2. What kind of name is Poon?

3. What does Fletch order to eat and drink his first time at the California Racquet Club?

4. Why did Fletch decide not to buy Alan Stanwyk's (Tim Matheson) house?

5. Which of the following is an alias Fletch did *not* use?

a) Don Corleone   b) Ted Nugent   c) Gordon Liddy   d) Arnold Babar
e) Jon Cocktolstoy   f) none of the above

Ferris Bueller's Day Off

1. Who does Ferris (Matthew Broderick) pretend to be to gain a lunch reservation at a posh restaurant?

2. What did Ferris get for his birthday instead of a car?

3. On what topic does Ferris have a test that day?

4. Which actor plays the drug dealer in the police station?

5. What is the principal's name?

Fletch

1. the Beatles' White Album, a cup of hot fat, and the head of Alfredo Garcia

2. Comanche Indian

3. "A Bloody Mary and a . . . steak sandwich."

4. "Came this close to buying this place. Then I found out Hopalong Cassidy killed himself here, blew it for me. . . . Bow and arrow, very weird."

5. f) none of the above

Ferris Beuller's Day Off

1. Abe Froman, the Sausage King of Chicago

2. a computer

3. European socialism

4. Charlie Sheen

5. Ed Rooney

City Slickers

1. How much does Phil (Daniel Stern) say he hates his wife?

2. Where does the opening scene of the movie take place?

3. According to Barry Shalowitz (Josh Mostel) what is the perfect flavor of ice cream to follow a meal of sauteed sea bass, potatoes au gratin, and asparagus?

4. "Hi Curly, kill anyone today?" asks Mitch (Billy Crystal). How does Curly (Jack Palance) respond?

5. Which actress plays Bonnie, the only female guest at the dude ranch?

Bull Durham

1. Who, according to Annie (Susan Sarandon), does Walt Whitman play for?

2. What is the first lesson that Crash (Kevin Costner) gives to Nuke (Tim Robbins)?

3. On a trip to the mound, Crash tells Nuke not to strike everybody out. What does Crash have against strikeouts?

4. Who is the first batter Nuke faces in his professional debut?

5. What happens when a batter hits the big wooden bull behind the right-field fence in Durham stadium?

City Slickers

1. "If hate were people, I'd be China!"

2. the running of the bulls in Pamplona, Spain

3. rum raisin

4. "Day ain't over yet."

5. Helen Slater

Bull Durham

1. "He sorta pitches for the Cosmic All-Stars."

2. "Don't think. It can only hurt the ball club."

3. "Strikeouts are boring, besides that, they're fascist."

4. Willie Foster

5. He wins a free steak.

The Blues Brothers

1. Which actor plays Jake and which plays Elwood?

2. What is the name of the bar where The Good Ole Blues Brothers Boys Band have their first gig?

3. And what kind of music do they play there?

4. After getting in trouble with the police again, Elwood gives them a false address—1060 West Addison, Chicago. Who really lives there?

5. Why are Jake and Elwood "puttin' the band back together"?

The Godfather

1. Finish the quote: "Leave the gun . . ."

2. Which character mumbles these lines: "I am honored and grateful that you have invited me to your daughter's wedding . . . on the day of your daughter's wedding."

3. During the famous baptism scene, who plays the baby being baptized?

4. According to Tessio (Abe Vigoda), what does a fish and a bulletproof vest wrapped in brown paper mean?

5. The movie opens with the wedding of Vito's (Marlon Brando) only daughter. What actress plays her?

The Blues Brothers

1. John Belushi is Jake and Dan Aykroyd is Elwood.

2. Bob's Country Bunker

3. "We got both kinds. We got country and western."

4. The Chicago Cubs. It is the address of Wrigley Field.

5. to raise enough money to save the orphanage

The Godfather

1. "... take the cannoli."

2. Lucca Brazzi

3. Sofia Coppola, the daughter of the director

4. "It's a Sicilian message. It means Lucca Brazzi sleeps with fishes."

5. Talia Shire

Blazing Saddles

1. What is the name of the song Lili Von Shtupp (Madeline Kahn) sings during her show?

2. Gene Wilder plays a drunken gunfighter who used to be the fastest gun in the West. What name did he go by?

3. What is Sheriff Bart's (Cleavon Little) limit on Shnitzengrubens?

4. Which actor plays Mongo?

5. How does Sheriff Bart respond when his friend says, in surprise, "They said you was hung?"

Biloxi Blues

1. In order to avoid eating army food, Jerome (Matthew Broderick) claims it is a Jewish holiday. What holiday does he create and who celebrates it?

2. What's a "cracker"?

3. How does Jerome describe his first sexual experience?

4. Which actress plays Daisy, Jerome's love interest?

5. What is the name of Jerome's company's drill sergeant and what actor plays him?

Blazing Saddles

1. "I'm Tired"
2. the Waco Kid
3. fifteen
4. Alex Karras
5. "And they was right."

Biloxi Blues

1. "It's called El Malagwaina. It's for Spanish Jews."
2. somebody from Georgia
3. "Fine as wine, sorta chatty, know what I mean?"
4. Penelope Ann Miller
5. Merwin J. Toomey, played by Christopher Walken

Caddyshack

1. What two grasses does Carl (Bill Murray) use to form his own hybrid?

2. How does Ty (Chevy Chase) measure himself against other golfers?

3. Al Czervik (Rodney Dangerfield) sees a hat in the pro shop he doesn't like. What does he say about it?

4. When Carl was a caddy for the Dalai Lama, he didn't receive any money as a tip, but what was he promised instead?

5. What was the name of Ty's college roommate?

Back to School

1. Which actor plays Professor Turgenson?

2. According to Alan, the stodgy old economics professor, what do all men want?

3. Thorton Mellon (Rodney Dangerfield) asks his waitress to bring a pitcher of beer every seven minutes until when?

4. What is the name of Thorton's famous dive?

5. What actor plays Dean Martin?

Caddyshack

1. Kentucky Blue Grass and Northern California Sensimilla

2. "By height."

3. "This is the worst lookin' hat I ever saw. You buy a hat like this I bet you get a free bowl of soup . . . Oh, looks good on you, though."

4. He would receive total consciousness on his deathbed.

5. Mitch Cumstein

Back to School

1. Sam Kinison

2. They want women "to dress up as Wonder Woman, tie him up with a golden lariat, and force him to tell the truth."

3. "Until someone passes out, then bring one every ten minutes."

4. the Triple Lindy

5. Ned Beatty

National Lampoon's Animal House

1. What is Blutarski's grade-point average?

2. Otter (Tim Matheson) takes the group on a road trip and pretends he is Fawn Leibowitz's fiancé, but Fawn is dead. How did she die?

3. Finish this line: "If I was in your shoes I'd be, uh . . ."

4. "What are you majoring in?"

5. Just when the Delta House looks finished, Blutarski jumps up and says "Nothing is over till we decide it is." Then, to emphasize the point, he makes a historical analogy. What does he say?

When Harry Met Sally . . .

1. Harry (Billy Crystal) and Sally (Meg Ryan) first met in college. What school did they attend?

2. How does Marie (Carrie Fisher) describe to Sally the anthropologist that Harry was dating?

3. What was the title of Jess's (Bruno Kirby) article about pesto?

4. According to Harry, what are all men thinking after they have sex with a woman?

5. What song does Harry find himself singing in front of Ira?

National Lampoon's Animal House

1. 0.0

2. in a kiln explosion

3. ". . . leaving, what a good idea."

4. "Primitive cultures."

5. "Was it over when the Germans bombed Pearl Harbor?"

When Harry Met Sally . . .

1. the University of Chicago

2. "Thin, pretty, big tits. Your basic nightmare."

3. "Pesto is the quiche of the eighties."

4. "How long do I have to lie here and hold her before I can get up and go home?"

5. "The Surrey with the Fringe on Top," from the musical *Oklahoma!*

The Untouchables

1. What is the home address of police officer Malone (Sean Connery)?

2. According to Malone, what is the "Chicago Way" to get Capone?

3. When Malone and Ness (Kevin Costner) are interviewing George Stone (Andy Garcia), Malone calls him a "lying member of a no-good race." What does Stone say?

4. Who wrote the screenplay?

5. What are Malone's dying words?

This Is Spinal Tap

1. David St. Hubbins (Michael McKean) wants to write a rock musical about the life of Jack the Ripper. What title does he have in mind?

2. What is St. Hubbins the Saint of?

3. How did the band's first three drummers die?

4. Why do Spinal Tap's amps go to 11, according to Nigel (Christopher Guest)?

5. Who plays Artie Fufkin of Polymer Records?

The Untouchables

1. 1634 Racine

2. "He pulls a knife, you pull a gun. He sends one of yours to the hospital, you send one of his to the morgue."

3. "It's much better than you, you stinkin' Irish pig."

4. David Mamet

5. "What are you prepared to do?"

This Is Spinal Tap

1. *Saucy Jack*

2. quality footwear

3. The first died in a bizarre gardening accident. The second choked on vomit. The third spontaneously combusted.

4. "If we need that little extra push over the cliff."

5. Paul Shaffer

Stripes

1. What job did Russel Ziskey (Harold Ramis) have before he joined the army?

2. How much money does Ox (John Candy) spend to mud-wrestle with the ladies?

3. When the recruiting officer asks John (Bill Murray) and Russel if they are homosexual, how do they respond?

4. What is Psycho's real name?

5. Why does John say chicks dig him?

Monty Python and the Holy Grail

1. What must you count to before throwing the Holy Hand Grenade?

2. In order to determine if someone is a witch, what must she be weighed against?

3. What is the one word that makes The Knights Who Say "Nee!" cringe?

4. What is the first item King Arthur must procure to get around these Knights?

5. "What is the air speed of an unladen swallow?"

Stripes

1. He taught English as a Second Language.

2. $413.58

3. "You mean, like, flaming?" (John) "Nah, we're not homosexual, but we are willing to learn." (Russel)

4. Francis Sawyer

5. "Chicks dig me because I rarely wear underwear, and when I do, it's usually something unusual."

Monty Python and the Holy Grail

1. three—no more, no less

2. a duck

3. "It."

4. a shrubbery

5. "An African or European swallow?"

The Naked Gun: From the Files of Police Squad!

1. Frank (Leslie Nielsen) used to be afraid of his "big gun" going off, but he doesn't have that problem anymore. What does he do to prevent it?

2. Who was scheduled to sing the National Anthem at the Mariners vs. Angels game?

3. Frank has a few thoughts about some good ways to die. What are they?

4. What actor plays the villain in this movie?

5. What musical instrument did Frank buy his wife for her birthday?

A Few Good Men

1. Colonel Jessup (Jack Nicholson) asks after Danny's (Tom Cruise) father only to find out that the man passed away seven years ago. How does Jessup describe how he feels?

2. What is the four-word Marine code?

3. According to Colonel Jessup, what is the "best in life"?

4. What is a "Code Red"?

5. Who directed this movie?

The Naked Gun: From the Files of Police Squad!

1. He thinks about baseball.

2. Enrico Pallazo

3. "A parachute not opening, that's a way to die. Getting caught in the gears of a combine, having your nuts bit off by a Laplander, that's how I wanna go."

4. Ricardo Montalban

5. a harp

A Few Good Men

1. "Don't I feel like the fuckin' asshole?"

2. "Unit. Corps. God. Country."

3. "If you haven't gotten a blow job from a superior officer, well, you're just letting the best in life pass you by."

4. When a Marine is disciplined by his own unit, unofficially, for not performing up to proper standards.

5. Rob Reiner

Murder by Death

1. In which part of the house are the Charlestons staying?

2. Which five fictional detectives are being spoofed?

3. Lionel Twain is the host for this sleuthing weekend. Who plays him?

4. Twain is trying to prove that he is the world's greatest detective, but when he claims "I'm the greatest, I'm number one," Sam Diamond (Peter Falk) disagrees. What does he say?

5. Whodunit?

Midnight Run

1. What is the name of the agency that Walsh (Robert De Niro) works for?

2. In order to get some money, Walsh and the Duke (Charles Grodin) pretend to be on the trail of some counterfeiters. What do they call the test they use to determine if a bill is real?

3. Which actor plays mob boss Sarrano?

4. When the stewardess takes dinner orders on the plane back to L.A., the Duke doesn't want anything, so what does Walsh suggest?

5. What is the name of the FBI agent that is following Walsh, and what actor plays him?

Murder by Death

1. They are staying in Wang's wing.

2. Sam Spade, Charlie Chan, Miss Marple, Hercule Poirot, and the team of Nick and Nora Charles from the *Thin Man* series.

3. Truman Capote

4. "To me, you look like number two, know what I mean?"

5. the maid, played by Nancy Walker

Midnight Run

1. Mosconi Bail Bonds

2. the Litmus Configuration

3. Dennis Farina

4. "Well, why don't you get the lobster, 'cause then I can get a little surf 'n' turf action going."

5. Alonzo Mosley, played by Yaphet Kotto

History of the World Part One

1. Who is the narrator?

2. What is an Order de Fait, according to Torquemada (Mel Brooks)?

3. When the Count de Monet (Harvey Korman) tells the King (Mel Brooks) he looks like the Piss Boy, how does the King respond?

4. What does Comicus (Mel Brooks) say he does for a living?

5. While playing chess, the King invokes the King's Privilege of three moves to one. What are his three moves?

National Lampoon's Vacation

1. What is the name of the car the Griswalds take across country?

2. What is Eddie's (Randy Quaid) response to the question, "Real tomato ketchup, Eddie?"

3. What is the "old line" Christine Brinkley tells Clark (Chevy Chase) she expected him to use on her when they finally met?

4. Where do Eddie and Katherine live?

5. As the Griswalds cross the Mississippi, Clark rattles off a few nicknames for the river. What are they?

History of the World Part One

1. Orson Welles

2. "It's what you oughtn't to do, but you do anyway."

3. "And you look like a bucket of shit."

4. "I coalesce the vapor of human experience into a viable and logical comprehension."

5. "Knight jumps queen. Bishop jumps queen. Pawn jumps queen. Gangbang!"

National Lampoon's Vacation

1. Wagon Queen Family Truckster

2. "Nothing but the best."

3. "I thought you were going to say you were with the CIA."

4. Coolidge, Kansas

5. "The Mighty Mississippi, the Ole Miss, the Old Man."

Ghostbusters

1. When Jeanine (Annie Potts) threatens to quit the job of Ghostbusters secretary, Peter (Bill Murray) suggests two other careers for her. What are they?

2. What is the license plate number of the Ghostbustermobile?

3. Gozer the Traveler has appeared on earth as a large Tork and as a Giant Slor. How does he appear this time?

4. How does Louis (Rick Moranis) respond after Ray (Dan Aykroyd) tells him he was involved in one of the most prolific supernatural phenomena of all time?

5. Before they first use their jet packs, Igon (Harold Ramis) offers some safety advice. What is his "safety tip"?

Ghostbusters

1. a job in the food service or housekeeping industries

2. ECTO-1

3. the Stay Puft Marshmallow Man

4. "Felt great."

5. "Don't cross the streams. . . . It would be bad."

Part Three

A QUOTER'S
Paradise for Intermediates

This section separates the Monday morning quoters from those who have really been in the trenches. Success here will depend on having actually seen these movies.

1. "Take live tuna fish and feed 'em mayonnaise. This is good. Call Star-kist."

2. "When you stole that cow, and your friend tried to make it with the cow? I wanna party with you, cowboy."

3. "She's not a woman. She's the Terminator."

4. "Espresso? I make it myself right back there with a little lemon twist."

5. "Buck Melanoma. Maisy Russel's wart."

6. "I eat breakfast three hundred yards from four thousand Cubans who are trained to kill me, so don't think for one second, you can come down here, flash your badge, and make me nervous."

7. "I'd have to say, 'Asssphincter says what?' "

8. "What's so funny about Biggus Dickus?"

9. "Sydney, sit down, relax, have a sandwich, drink a glass of milk, do some fuckin' thing, will ya?"

10. "The tension in the air was so thick, you could cut it with a knife. Which is more than I could say for the liver."

11. "Women weaken legs."

1. Night Shift
   What two actors run the show down at the morgue?

2. Stripes
   What job did John (Bill Murray) have before he entered the army?

3. Throw Momma from the Train
   Who directed this 1987 movie?

4. Beverly Hills Cop
   Which actor plays the espresso-making Serge?

5. Uncle Buck
   Who directed this 1989 movie?

6. A Few Good Men
   True or false: Jack Nicholson won the 1992 Best Supporting Actor Oscar for his portrayal of Colonel Jessup?

7. Wayne's World
   In what city was *Wayne's World* filmed?

8. Monty Python's Life of Brian
   What is the name of the revolutionary group that Brian joins?

9. Midnight Run
   What excuse does the snitch in the bail bonds office use to sneak out when he leaks Jack's (Robert De Niro) whereabouts to the mob?

10. Brighton Beach Memoirs
    According to Jerome's (Jonathan Silverman) brother Stanley, why can't you marry your first cousin?

11. Rocky
    True or false: Stallone won the Best Actor Oscar for this flick?

ANSWERS TO BONUS QUESTIONS

1. Henry Winkler and Michael Keaton
2. He was a taxi driver.
3. Danny DeVito
4. Bronson Pinchot
5. John Hughes
6. False. Gene Hackman won that year for his performance in *Unforgiven*. Nicholson won in 1983 for *Terms of Endearment*.
7. Aurora, Illinois
8. the People's Front of Judea
9. He says he's going out for doughnuts.
10. "You can't marry your first cousin, you get babies with nine heads."
11. False. The film won Oscars for Best Film and Best Director in 1976.

12. "Pain is such a rush."

13. "Why don't you run outside and jerk yourself a soda?"

14. "Yeah, well I guess they had it comin'."
"We all have it comin', kid."

15. "Owww! I thought you said your dog didn't bite?"
"That is not my dog."

16. "Tell me something, my friend—you ever dance with the devil in the pale moonlight?"

17. "I'm tired. I've been under a lot of stress. I lost my wife, I lost my job, and I've got some sort of rash from making in the bushes!"

18. "There's such a fine line between stupid and clever."

19. "So what do you think? Is that him?"
"Nah. Those fellas are all gone now."

20. "You're not my kinda cop, but you're smart and you smell good. You're not a pansy, I know that, but what the hell are ya?"

21. "One of them manure spreaders jackknifed on the Santa Ana, god-awful mess. You should see my shoes."

22. "I'm not talkin' about treasure boatin' or game sailin'. I'm talkin' about sharkin'."

12. Bachelor Party
    "Is that the foot-long?"

13. Bugsy
    Who are the two stars of this movie?

14. Unforgiven
    Little Bill (Gene Hackman) is the sheriff of what town?

15. The Pink Panther Strikes Again
    What is Inspector Clouseau (Peter Sellers) searching for in this sequel?

16. Batman
    What is the Joker's real name?

17. City Slickers
    How old was the checkout girl Phil (Daniel Stern) slept with?

18. This Is Spinal Tap
    What color is the cover of the band's new album, *Smell the Glove?*

19. Eight Men Out
    Which team did the White Sox play in the 1919 World Series?

20. Murder by Death
    What does Mr. Wang (Peter Sellers) think of Mr. Charleston's (David Niven) theory about the murderer's identity?

21. Fletch
    Where is the Records Room?

22. Jaws
    Who wrote the 1974 novel on which this movie was based?

ANSWERS TO BONUS QUESTIONS

12. "And then some."
13. Warren Beatty as Bugsy Siegel and Annette Bening as Virginia Hill
14. Big Whiskey, Wyoming
15. Clouseau is searching not for the famous diamond, The Pink Panther, but his boss gone mad, Chief Inspector Dreyfus (Herbert Lom).
16. Jack Napier
17. She was twenty.
18. black
19. the Cincinnati Reds
20. "It stupid. It most stupid theory I ever heard."
21. B-1
22. Peter Benchley

23. "We'll never be sick, we won't get any older, and we won't ever die."

24. "Into the mud, scum queen."

25. "When there was no crawdaddy to be found, we ate sand."
"You ate sand?"
"We ate sand."

26. "Yo, later for you, Bathead. . . . You ain't no actor, man, that's all special effects."

27. "Didn't you notice on the plane when you started talking, eventually I started reading the vomit bag?"

28. "Your mother so poor, I seen her kicking a can down the street, I said, 'What ya doin?' She said, 'Movin.' "

29. "Do you mean sleep over?"
"Well, yeah."
"Okay, but I get to be on top."

30. "Interesting broad. Where'd she develop her personality, a car crash?"

31. "Anything travels that far oughta have a damn stewardess on it, don't ya think?"

32. "Well, the cat has dragged in a sight for four eyes, that's for sure."

23. Cocoon
Which actor won an Oscar for this film?

24. The Man with Two Brains
What is the name of the brain? (Can you spell it?)

25. Raising Arizona
When the baby was stolen, he was wearing pajamas. What did they look like, according to Nathan Arizona (Trey Wilson)?

26. Hollywood Shuffle
What is the name of the TV star "Bathead's" sitcom?

27. Planes, Trains and Automobiles
Which actor cameos as the guy Neal (Steve Martin) races for a cab at the beginning of the movie?

28. White Men Can't Jump
What former NBA star plays Raymond, the gun-wielding playground basketball player?

29. Big
What is the name of the carnival game that grants Josh Baskin (Tom Hanks) his wish?

30. About Last Night
"Was she a pro?"

31. Bull Durham
In which of the following does Crash (Kevin Costner) not believe? a) the sweet spot b) high fiber c) the soul d) the hanging curve ball e) hard-core pornography f) none of the above

32. Short Circuit
What is the robot's name?

ANSWERS TO BONUS QUESTIONS

23. Don Ameche won the Oscar for Best Supporting Actor in 1985 for his role as Art, the senior citizen who finds the fountain of youth.
24. Anne Uumellmahaye
25. "I don't know, they were jammies. They had Yodas and shit on 'em."
26. *There's a Bat in My House*
27. Kevin Bacon
28. Marques Johnson
29. Zoltar
30. "At this point, we don't know."
31. e) hard-core pornography. He believes in soft-core pornography.
32. Number 5

33. "Beware of the dwarf."

34. "You know what word I'm not comfortable with? 'Nuance.' "

35. "Supreme executive power derives from a mandate from the masses, not from some farcical aquatic ceremony."

36. "It's puberty . . . you never heard that word before? Don't you read books?"
"Yeah, *The Count of Monte Cristo.* It never mentioned puberty."

37. "Except for socially, you're my role model."

38. "She had the kind of legs you'd like to suck on for a day."

39. "You see how it works is, the train moves, not the station."

40. "Let justice be done though the heavens fall."

41. "Hey buddy, you got a dead cat in there or what?"
"Fuck you, asshole."

42. "I got it, I got it, I got it! I ain't got it!"

33. Foul Play
Which actor plays the landlord, Mr. Hennesey?

34. Diner
This is the first of a trilogy of films by Barry Levinson. Name the other two.

35. Monty Python and the Holy Grail
Finish the quote: "Well, she turned me into a newt . . ."

36. Brighton Beach Memoirs
"How horny can you get?"

37. Broadcast News
Which actress says this line?

38. The Naked Gun: From the Files of Police Squad
What does Frank (Leslie Nielsen) say his policy is when he sees five weirdos in togas stabbing a guy in the park?

39. A League of Their Own
What prayer does Jimmy Dugan (Tom Hanks) say in the clubhouse before the final game?

40. JFK
For what city was Jim Garrison (Kevin Costner) the District Attorney?

41. The Terminator
What responses does the Terminator's (Arnold Schwarzenegger) computer have to this question?

42. High Anxiety
To what director is this movie an homage?

ANSWERS TO BONUS QUESTIONS

33. Burgess Meredith
34. *Tin Men* (1987) and *Avalon* (1990)
35. ". . . I got better."
36. "I don't know. What's the high score?"
37. Joan Cusack
38. "I shoot the bastards, that's my policy."
39. "Lord, hallowed by thy name. May our feet be swift, may our bats be mighty, and may our balls be plentiful."

40. New Orleans
41. *Yes/No*
Or what?
Go away
Please come back later
Fuck you
42. Alfred Hitchcock

43. "I shall walk through the Valley of the Shadow of Death. In fact, I shall run through the Valley of the Shadow of Death, 'cause you get out of the valley quicker that way."

44. "Never got me down, Ray. Hear me? You never got me down."

45. "You. My room. Ten-thirty tonight. You. Ten forty-five. Bring a friend."

46. "Where does he get those wonderful toys?"

47. "You're a little monkey woman. You're lean and you're mean, and you're not too far between, either, I'll bet."

48. "It's *Out of Africa* meets *Pretty Woman.*"

49. "I just wish there was a way I could vote for you a hundred times." "There is, actually. . . . Just kidding."

50. "I'm black, and I'm proud."

51. "I was born a poor black child."

52. "Get me Ham on five, hold the Mayo."

53. "I'm your density."

43. Love and Death
True or false: Woody Allen acted in and wrote this film, but did not direct it?

44. Raging Bull
Who is "Ray"?

45. Robin Hood: Prince of Thieves
Which actor plays the Sheriff of Nottingham?

46. Batman
What does Vicki Vale (Kim Basinger) do for a living?

47. Caddyshack
Judge Smails (Ted Knight) tells Ty (Chevy Chase), "[Dr. Beeper is] club champion and I'm no slouch myself." What is Ty's response?

48. The Player
What is the name of the movie-within-the-movie starring Bruce Willis and Julia Roberts?

49. Bob Roberts
In what state is Bob Roberts running for senator?

50. The Commitments
Where are the boys and girls in the band from?

51. The Jerk
According to Navin (Steve Martin), what restaurant serves the best pizza in a cup?

52. Airplane
What is the flight number?

53. Back to the Future
How much energy is needed to send Marty (Michael J. Fox) back to the future?

ANSWERS TO BONUS QUESTIONS

43. False. He also directed.
44. Sugar Ray Robinson
45. Alan Rickman
46. She's a professional photographer.
47. "Don't sell yourself short, Judge, you're a tremendous slouch."
48. *Habeas Corpus*
49. Pennsylvania
50. Dublin, Ireland
51. Cup o' Pizza
52. Flight 209
53. "1.21 Jiggiwatts"

54. "You wanna play games? Say hello to my little friend."

55. "But the servant waits, while the masturbates."

56. "Oh, come right in. Don't let the fact that my door is closed dissuade you in any way from entering my office."

57. "This is the one time where television really fails to capture the true excitement of a large squirrel predicting the weather."

58. "We have no tower, sir."
"No tower? Why the hell aren't I notified about these things?"

59. "Why can't we pick our own colors?"
"No way, no way. Tried it once, it doesn't work. You get four guys all fightin' over who's gonna be Mr. Black."

60. "I'll be taking these Huggies and whatever cash you got."

61. "It's a shark. . . . And I know what a shark looks like, because I've seen one up close."

62. "They have decided the album cover is sexist."
"So what? What's wrong with being sexy?"

63. "How can you describe poetry like *American Bandstand?* Oh, I like Byron, I give him a forty-two, but I can't dance to it."

64. "Sometimes nothin' can be a pretty cool hand."

54. Scarface
Tony Montana (Al Pacino) loves Miami. What does he compare that town to?

55. History of the World Part One
What is the name of Josephus's (Gregory Hines) sand dance?

56. Beverly Hills Cop II
What actor plays the lawyer Sydney Bernstein?

57. Groundhog Day
What trick did Needlenose Ned do at the high school talent show?

58. Airplane II: The Sequel
What actor plays the man in charge of Alpha Beta Lunar Base?

59. Reservoir Dogs
What radio show is playing throughout this movie?

60. Raising Arizona
What character does Randall "Tex" Cobb play?

61. Jaws 2
How does Brody (Roy Scheider) kill the shark this time?

62. This Is Spinal Tap
According to the band, why do young women run screaming when they see them up close?

63. Dead Poets Society
What is the name of the boarding school where Mr. Keating (Robin Williams) teaches?

64. Cool Hand Luke
How many eggs does Luke (Paul Newman) eat in an hour?

ANSWERS TO BONUS QUESTIONS

54. "This town is like a great big pussy just waiting to get fucked."
55. the Ethiopian Shim Sham
56. Gilbert Gottfried
57. the whistling belly button trick
58. William Shatner
59. *K-Billy's Super Sounds of the Seventies*
60. Leonard Smalls
61. He electrocutes it.
62. "We've got armadillos in our trousers. It's quite frightening."
63. Welton
64. fifty

65. "Get me the president on the horn."

66. "I'd buy that for a dollar!"

67. "I'm funny how? I mean funny like I'm a clown, I amuse you? . . . Funny how? How am I funny?"

68. "Her big move should be coming up any moment—the combination hair flip with a giggle."

69. "Stay where you are, everybody. I gotta go to the can and I don't wanna miss nothin'."

70. "About six feet tall?"
"Six-five."
"Dark brown hair?"
"Light colored."
"Sounds like our man."

71. "Back off, man, I'm a scientist."

72. "Well, when an adult male is chasing a female with intent to commit rape, I shoot the bastard, that's my policy."

73. "Yo, put some extra mozzarella on that motherfuckin' shit."

74. "Kato is in hospital. It nearly blew his little yellow skin off."

65. War Games
What does W.O.P.R stand for?

66. Robocop
What actor plays the Robocop?

67. GoodFellas
Who played Tommy's (Joe Pesci) mom in this movie?

68. About Last Night
What is the degree of difficulty on the maneuver described?

69. Murder by Death
Which detective solves the crime correctly?

70. Midnight Run
What does Jack (Robert De Niro) yell out in the airport to let the Feds know it's time to move in on Sarrano?

71. Ghostbusters
What sponge cake does Igon (Harold Ramis) use to describe the amount of negative supernatural energy present in the city?

72. Dirty Harry
How does Harry (Clint Eastwood) respond when the police commissioner asks him how he established the intent to commit rape?

73. Do the Right Thing
How much money does Mookie make working at the pizzeria?

74. The Return of the Pink Panther
If the bellboy keeps up the good work, what does Clouseau say he will do for him?

ANSWERS TO BONUS QUESTIONS

65. War Operation Plan Response
66. Peter Weller
67. director Martin Scorsese's mother, Catherine
68. 3.2
69. none of them
70. "Sarrano's got the disks!"
71. a Twinkie

72. "When a naked man is chasing a woman with a butcher's knife and a hard-on, I figure he's not out collecting for the Red Cross."
73. $250 a week
74. "I will see to it that you become a bell man."

75. "Counselor. Come out, come out wherever you are."

76. "A king without his sword. A land without a king."

77. "Mo' Better makes it mo' better."

78. "Cancel the kitchen scraps for lepers and orphans, no more merciful be-headings, and call off Christmas."

79. "Bruno is almost blind, has to operate wholly by touch. Klaus is a moron who knows only what he reads in the *New York Post*."

80. "Stack 'em, pack 'em, and rack 'em."

81. "What are you lookin' at, butthead?"

82. "You ever fight a dinosaur, kid? They can cause a variety of damage."

83. "You just keep on thinking, Butch, that's what you're good at."

84. "What do you see when you're in the dark and the demons come?"
"I see you, Frank. I see you standing over the grave of another dead president."

85. "They used to call me Crazy Joe, well, now they can call me Batman."

75. Cape Fear
    For what crime has Max Cady (Robert De Niro) just served a jail sentence?

76. Excalibur
    What is the charm of making?

77. Mo' Better Blues
    Why does Giant (Spike Lee) bet the Pirates in a doubleheader over the Mets?

78. Robin Hood: Prince of Thieves
    What is Robin Hood's real name?

79. Top Secret!
    What actor plays Nick Rivers?

80. Die Hard 2
    What actor plays Carmine, the airport's police captain?

81. Back to the Future
    What kind of car does Doc use to build his time machine?

82. Rocky III
    What is Clubber Lang's (Mr. T) prediction for his fight with Rocky?

83. Butch Cassidy and the Sundance Kid
    What is the last line in the movie, said just before Butch and Sundance go out to battle the entire Bolivian Army?

84. In the Line of Fire
    What was John F. Kennedy's favorite poem, according to Booth (John Malkovich)?

85. Lean on Me
    Crazy Joe (Morgan Freeman) is the principal of what high school?

ANSWERS TO BONUS QUESTIONS

75. He has just served fourteen years for rape.
76. spelled phonetically, "Annal Nathrak, Ulfas Bethard, Dothiel Dienvay"
77. "Mets need more black ball players."
78. Robin of Locksley
79. Val Kilmer
80. Dennis Franz
81. a DeLorean
82. "Pain."
83. "For a moment there, I thought we were in trouble."
84. "His favorite poem was 'I Have a Rendezvous with Death,' which is not a good poem."
85. Eastside High School

86. "Remember, Sully, when I promised to kill you last? I lied."

87. "Be afraid. Be very afraid."

88. "Once you have a man with no legs, you never go back."

89. "Did you see that bodacious set of ta-tas?"

90. "Any friend of Wendell's is a friend of mine."

91. "They was givin' me ten thousand watts a day and I'm hot to trot. Next woman that takes me on is gonna light up like a pinball machine and pay off in silver dollars."

92. "Blessed are the cheesemakers."

93. "What about the bridge?"
"That ain't a bridge, that's pre-Columbian art."

94. "You got that big 'Z' in your fro. Hey man, what are you, the black Zorro?"

95. "We're gonna need a bigger boat."

86. Commando
What actress plays John Matrix's (Arnold Schwarzenegger) daughter, Jenny?

87. The Fly
Which actor plays the fly in the remake?

88. Trading Places
When Billy Ray (Eddie Murphy) is released from jail, he is walking down the steps of the precinct, and a policeman is having a bit of trouble with a criminal. What friendly advice does Billy Ray give the officer?

89. An Officer and a Gentleman
According to Sergeant Foley (Louis Gossett, Jr.), what are the only two things that come out of Oklahoma?

90. Fraternity Vacation
What actor plays Mother?

91. One Flew over the Cuckoo's Nest
What happens to McMurphy (Jack Nicholson) at the end of the movie?

92. Monty Python's Life of Brian
"All right, but apart from sanitation, medicine, education, wine, public order, irrigation, the fresh water system, and public health. What have the Romans ever done for us?"

93. Romancing the Stone
According to the map, where is the stone located?

94. White Men Can't Jump
What is a quint?

95. Jaws
What is the name of Quint's (Robert Shaw) boat?

ANSWERS TO BONUS QUESTIONS

86. Alyssa Milano
87. Jeff Goldblum
88. "May I suggest using your nightstick, Officer?"
89. "Steers and queers."
90. Tim Robbins

91. McMurphy is lobotomized by the hospital, then suffocated by the Chief.
92. "Brought peace?"
93. El Corazón
94. the forbidden fruit in the garden of Eden
95. *Orca*

Part Four

THEY SAID IT
Lines from Hollywood's Stars

Bill Murray

1. "The power grid was shut off by dickless here."
   "Is this true?"
   "Yes, it's true. This man has no dick."

2. "Barnekey? He still owes me money!"

3. "I'd keep playing. I don't think the heavy stuff's gonna come down for quite a while."

4. "He's ugly. I mean he's not Elephant Man ugly, but he's not attractive . . . and he stinks."

5. "But more important than the score of this game is to score at the big social at our place tonight."

6. "I don't suppose there's any possibility of getting an espresso or cappuccino this morning?"
   "Oh, I don't know. . . ."
   ". . . How to spell espresso or cappucino."

7. "I can't get the antlers glued on to this little guy."
   "Have you tried staples?"

8. "I wish I had a theater that was only open when it rained."

Bill Murray

1. Ghostbusters
   Dr. Venkman has two doctorates. In what fields are they?

2. Stripes
   What does John call his inventive sexual technique, which involves the use of a spatula?

3. Caddyshack
   What is Carl's job title?

4. Ghostbusters II
   According to one of Dr. Venkman's guests on *World of the Psychic*, the world is going to end. What day does he say is the final day?

5. Meatballs
   What is the name of the rival camp?

6. Groundhog Day
   What song does Phil wake up to on Groundhog Day?

7. Scrooged
   What is the name of the network that Frank Cross works for?

8. Tootsie
   What actress won an Oscar for her performance in this 1982 film?

ANSWERS TO BONUS QUESTIONS

1. psychology and parapsychology
2. the Aunt Jemima Treatment
3. Assistant Greenskeeper
4. "Valentine's Day—bummer."
5. Camp Mohawk
6. "I Got You, Babe"
7. ICB
8. Jessica Lange won the Oscar for Best Supporting Actress.

Al Pacino

1. "Fredo, you're my older brother and I love you, but don't ever take sides against the family again—ever."

2. "You gotta make the money first. Then when you make the money, then you get the power. Then when you get the power, then you get the women."

3. "I want it wall to wall with John Daniels."
   "Don't you mean Jack Daniels?"
   "He may be Jack to you, son, but when you've known him as long as I have . . . that's a joke."

4. "I know it was you, Fredo. You broke my heart. You broke my heart."

5. "Wait a minute, I'm having a thought. Oh yes, I'm gonna have a thought. It's coming . . . it's gone."

Al Pacino

1. The Godfather
True or false: Al Pacino's performance in this film won the Academy Award for Best Supporting Actor in 1972?

2. Scarface
Which actress plays Tony Montana's (Pacino) sister?

3. Scent of a Woman
What military rank is Frank Slade?

4. The Godfather Part II
Corleone was not Vito's (Marlon Brando) real last name. Where did that name come from?

5. Dick Tracy
What character does Pacino play in this film?

ANSWERS TO BONUS QUESTIONS

1. False. Joel Grey won that year for *Cabaret*.
2. Mary Elizabeth Mastrantonio
3. lieutenant colonel
4. It was the name of the town he was from in Sicily.
5. Big Boy Caprice

Eddie Murphy

1. "Is there a problem, Officers?"

2. "That's seven bucks, buddy."
   "For a Coke? I can get blown for seven dollars."

3. "I don't like white people. I hate rednecks. You people are rednecks."

4. "The royal penis is clean, Your Highness."

5. "Tell Victor that . . . Ramone went to the clinic today . . . and I think Victor should go check himself out . . . before things start falling off the man."

Eddie Murphy

1. Trading Places

   While in jail, Billy Ray Valentine (Murphy) pretends to be a karate pro. What special technique does he demonstrate?

2. Beverly Hills Cop II

   What alias does Axel Foley (Murphy) use when he pretends to be a psychic from the island of St. Croix?

3. 48 Hours

   What is the name of the redneck bar in which this scene takes place?

4. Coming to America

   What country is Murphy the prince of, and what actor plays the king?

5. Beverly Hills Cop

   Who is the subject of the article that Axel Foley is supposedly writing for *Rolling Stone* magazine?

ANSWERS TO BONUS QUESTIONS

1. "That's called the quart of blood technique. You do that, a quart of blood will drop out the person's body."
2. Johnny Wishbone
3. Torchy's
4. Zamunda. James Earl Jones plays the king.
5. Michael Jackson

Steve Martin

1. "There's something I want to say that's always been difficult for me to say—I slit the sheet, the sheet I slit, and on the slitted sheet I sit."

2. "Would you like a drink?"
   "Please . . . Tahitian Lady."
   "Flaming?"
   "No, that's for tourists."

3. "Farley, farley, farley, farley, farley, farley—Hafar!"

4. "I really admire your shoes . . . and as much as I'd like to have a pair just like them, I really wouldn't want to be in your shoes at this particular time and place."

5. "By the way, when you're telling these little stories, here's a good idea—have a point."

6. "Half double decaffeinated half-caf. With a twist of lemon.".

7. "Oklahoma! Oklahoma! Oklahoma! Oklahoma!"

Steve Martin

1. The Jerk
   Which actor plays Mr. Hartooney, the gas station owner?

2. The Man with Two Brains
   How do you spell Martin's character's last name?

3. ¡Three Amigos!
   In the beginning of the movie, we meet Mr. Flugelman, the president of the studio that makes the *Three Amigo* movies. What actor plays him, and who plays his two assistants?

4. Roxanne
   What is CD's (Martin) occupation?

5. Planes, Trains and Automobiles
   What city do Del (John Candy) and Neal (Martin) leave from, and where are they going?

6. L.A. Story
   What character does Sarah Jessica Parker play?

7. Dirty Rotten Scoundrels
   What is the name of the Riviera town where Freddie (Martin) and Lawrence (Michael Caine) are fighting for the right to work?

ANSWERS TO BONUS QUESTIONS

1. Jackie Mason
2. "Just like it sounds. Hfuhruhurr."
3. Joe Mantegna plays Flugelman. Jon Lovitz and Phil Hartman are his sidekicks.
4. the fire chief
5. They leave from New York bound for Chicago.
6. SanDeE☆
7. Beaumont Sur Mer

Tom Cruise

1. "You got authorization from Aunt Jenny?"

2. "Do I have 'Fuck me' written on my forehead?"
"I can't see a thing without my contacts."

3. "It's classified. I could tell you, but then I'd have to kill you."

4. "Sometimes you gotta say 'What the fuck'—make your move."

5. "It's like a nightmare, isn't it? Just keeps getting worse and worse."

6. "Disappointed? Why should I be disappointed? I got the rose bushes, didn't I? I got a used car didn't I?"

Tom Cruise
1. A Few Good Men
   According to Colonel Jessup (Jack Nicholson), what is the only type of danger?

2. Cocktail
   Which actor plays Brian's (Cruise) mentor?

3. Top Gun
   What team wins the Top Gun trophy?

4. Risky Business
   What school does Joel (Cruise) interview for and get into?

5. The Color of Money
   Who directed this flick?

6. Rain Man
   What model car does Babbit (Cruise) inherit?

ANSWERS TO BONUS QUESTIONS

1. "Grave danger."
2. Brian Brown
3. Ice Man and Slider
4. Princeton University
5. Martin Scorsese
6. 1949 Buick Roadmaster Straight 8 ("Fireball 8")

Billy Crystal

1. "Have you ever noticed the older you get, the younger your girlfriends get? Soon you'll be dating sperm."

2. "Mime is money."

3. "Thank you so much for bringing up such a painful subject. While you're at it, why don't you give me a nice paper cut and pour lemon juice on it?"

4. "Three huge guys, one of them wearing a T-shirt that says 'Don't Fuck With Mr. Zero'."

5. "Class dismissed. I have an enormous headache in my eye."

6. "Mother? Mother? Can I have some more petit marshmallows in my hot cocoa?"

7. "I have done you a million favors, and one time I ask you to do something for me . . ."
"Oh yeah, and the one time is sucking poison out of your friend's ass."

Billy Crystal

1. City Slickers
   Guys talk about baseball, girls talk about relationships. According to Ed (Bruno Kirby), which topic is better?

2. This Is Spinal Tap
   Crystal has a great cameo in this film, but another famous actor also makes a cameo as a mime. Who is it?

3. The Princess Bride
   Which actress plays Miracle Max's (Crystal) wife?

4. When Harry Met Sally . . .
   Where does this scene take place?

5. Throw Momma from the Train
   Who plays Larry's (Crystal) friend Lester?

6. Running Scared
   What's the answer to the Bible question?

7. City Slickers II: The Legend of Curly's Gold
   What's Curly's (Jack Palance) brother's name?

ANSWERS TO BONUS QUESTIONS

1. "No contest, we win . . . if that were as interesting as baseball, they'd have cards for it and sell it with gum."
2. Dana Carvey
3. Carol Kane
4. during a Giants game at the Meadowlands
5. Branford Marsalis
6. Deuteronomy
7. Duke Washburn

John Candy

1. "Excuse me, stewardess, is there a movie on this flight?"

2. "They printed my letter in the 'Forum' section. The story's entitled, 'Lesbian No More.' "

3. "I'm a Mog. Half man, half dog. I'm my own best friend."

4. "Here's a quarter. Go downtown and have a rat gnaw that thing off your face."

5. "I am Dujour Delioche."
   "Can you spell that?"
   "I don't think so. Try it with a 'D.' "

6. "Do you feel this vehicle is safe for highway travel?"
   "Yes, I do. Yes, I really do."

John Candy

1. Stripes
   What is Candy's character's name?

2. Splash
   What magazine has the "Forum" section?

3. Spaceballs
   What actor plays Yogurt?

4. Uncle Buck
   What actor plays Buck's (Candy) nephew, Miles Russel?

5. Who's Harry Crumb?
   What actress plays the villainess?

6. Planes, Trains and Automobiles
   What does Del (Candy) do for a living?

ANSWERS TO BONUS QUESTIONS

1. Dewey Oxberger
2. *Penthouse* magazine
3. Mel Brooks
4. Macaulay Culkin
5. Annie Potts
6. He sells shower curtain rings.

Danny DeVito

1. "Not only are we kidnappers, but I'm about to have a close encounter with a cattle prod."

2. "Well, Ralph, Debbie can't come to the phone right now, my dick's in her mouth. How about if I have her call you back when I'm done?"

3. "Owen loves his momma!"

4. "Ya bolted outta nowhere, pal!"
   "I bolted? At six miles per hour I bolted into the street?"

5. "You lousy minx, I oughta have you spayed."

6. "Were you nervous the first time?"
   "I was twelve years old and she was a nun. Talk about pressure."

Danny DeVito

1. Romancing the Stone
   Who directed this movie?

2. Ruthless People
   What actress plays Sam Stone's (DeVito) wife?

3. Throw Momma from the Train
   What Hitchcock movie does Owen (DeVito) go to see and then try and imitate?

4. Tin Men
   What are "tin men"?

5. Batman Returns
   What is the Penguin's real name?

6. Twins
   What are the two brothers' (DeVito and Arnold Shwarzenegger) names?

ANSWERS TO BONUS QUESTIONS

1. Robert Zemeckis
2. Bette Midler
3. *Strangers on a Train*
4. people who sell aluminum siding
5. Oswold Cobblepot
6. Vincent and Julius

Robert De Niro

1. "He's a pretty kid, too. I mean, I don't know, I got a problem. Should I fuck 'em or fight 'em?"

2. "I want that SOB dead. . . . I want his house burned to the ground. I wanna go there in the middle of the night, I wanna piss on his ashes."

3. "These sunglasses, they're really nice. Are they government issue or do all you guys go, like, to the same store to get them?"

4. "You're gonna learn about loss."

5. "Hey, Marie! Get in the fucking car!"
   "No."
   "Come on, baby, you know I love you . . . get in the fucking car!"

Robert De Niro

1. Raging Bull
   Which actor played Jake's (De Niro) brother Joey LaMotta?

2. The Untouchables
   Who was Al Capone's (De Niro) number-one hit man?

3. Midnight Run
   Which actor plays the Duke?

4. Cape Fear
   Which three actors from the original (1962) version of *Cape Fear* also appear in this remake?

5. A Bronx Tale
   One of the local hoods was called Mush by the local mafioso. Why?

ANSWERS TO BONUS QUESTIONS

1. Joe Pesci
2. Frank Nitti
3. Charles Grodin
4. Robert Mitchum, Gregory Peck, and Martin Balsam
5. "We called him Eddie Mush because everything he touched turned to mush."

Mel Brooks

1. "What in the wide, wide world of sports is a goin' on here?"

2. "Don't get saucy with me, Bernaise."

3. "A week? Are you kidding? This play has to close on page four."

4. "Werewolf?"
"There wolf. There castle."

5. "What's the matter, Colonel Sanders? Chicken?"

6. "Dinner is served promptly at eight in the private dining room. Those who are late do not get fruit cup."

7. "No!"

Mel Brooks

1. Blazing Saddles
   What is the name of the town in jeopardy?

2. History of the World Part One
   What character does Harvey Korman play?

3. The Producers
   What is the name of the play Max (Zero Mostel) and Leo (Gene Wilder) put on?

4. Young Frankenstein
   What happens everytime someone says "Frau Blucher"?

5. Spaceballs
   Name the character who is modeled after *Star Wars'* Jabba the Hut.

6. High Anxiety
   What is the name of the mental institution?

7. Silent Movie
   Who speaks this, the only word in the film?

ANSWERS TO BONUS QUESTIONS

1. Rock Ridge
2. the Count De Monet
3. *Springtime for Hitler*
4. Horses whinny.
5. Pizza the Hut
6. the Psychoneurotic Institute for the Very, Very Nervous
7. Marcel Marceau

Dustin Hoffman

1. "I'm walkin' here! I'm walkin' here!"

2. "We're looking for somebody shorter."
   "I can be shorter."

3. "I want to say one word to you. Just one word. Are you listening? Plastics!"

4. "Shut the fuck up, Lou. You're ugly and you're dumb and that's the truth of you."

5. "I'm an excellent driver."

Dustin Hoffman
1. Midnight Cowboy
   What is Hoffman's character's name?

2. Tootsie
   What actor/director played Michael's (Hoffman) agent?

3. The Graduate
   For whom did this film win the Best Director Oscar?

4. Billy Bathgate
   What gangster does Hoffman play?

5. Rain Man
   What is the slogan of the radio station 97-X?

ANSWERS TO BONUS QUESTIONS

1. Ratso Rizzo
2. Sydney Pollack
3. Mike Nichols
4. Dutch Schulz
5. "97-X BAM! The Future of Rock and Roll."

Dan Aykroyd

1. "We came, we saw, we kicked its ass."

2. "Bring me four fried chickens and a Coke."
   "And some dry white toast."

3. "Looking good, Billy Ray."
   "Feeling good, Louis."

4. "Just the facts, if you don't mind, ma'am."

5. "I was probing to determine skeletal girth and muscle tone. It's a new technique. We mock what we don't understand."

Dan Aykroyd

1. Ghostbusters
   True or false: Ray is the character who summons the Stay Puft Marshmallow Man?

2. The Blues Brothers
   What midwestern fascist group joins the chase after the Blues Brothers at the end of the movie?

3. Trading Places
   In what commodity do the boys (Aykroyd and Eddie Murphy) make their fortune?

4. Dragnet
   Friday (Aykroyd) saves and falls in love with what character?

5. Spies Like Us
   What singer performs this movie's title theme song?

ANSWERS TO BONUS QUESTIONS

1. true
2. the Illinois Nazis
3. frozen concentrated orange juice
4. the virgin Connie Swayle
5. Paul McCartney

Gene Hackman

1. "Me, a poor blind man, and you a mute—an incredibly big mute."

2. "Revenge. We will kill the son of our jailer."
   "Revenge!"
   "Revenge! Now we're cooking, huh?"

3. "Well, a lot of folks did call him Two Gun, but that wasn't because he was sporting two pistols."

4. "You like baseball, do ya, Mr. Anderson?"
   "Yeah, I do. You know, it's the only time when a black man can wave a stick at a white man and not start a riot."

5. "Otisberg? Otisberg?"

6. "The Lord. I can feel his strength."
   "Well, keep your strength in the dribble, all right?"

Gene Hackman

1. Young Frankenstein
   Which actor plays the Monster?

2. Superman II
   What does Lex Luthor want in exchange for helping Zod?

3. Unforgiven
   English Bob (Richard Harris) is having a book written about him called *The Duke of Death*. What does Little Bill (Hackman) call it?

4. Mississippi Burning
   What has four eyes and still can't see?

5. Superman
   Lex Luthor has two hydrogen bombs. One is going to destroy California. Where is the other headed?

6. Hoosiers
   What is the name of the school where Hackman is the coach?

ANSWERS TO BONUS QUESTIONS

1. Peter Boyle
2. Australia
3. *The Duck of Death*
4. Mississippi
5. Hackensack, New Jersey
6. Hickory

Chevy Chase

1. "I wonder if you could tell me how to get back on the expressway?"
   "Hey, fuck yo momma."

2. "Why don't you guys go down to the gym and pump each other."

3. "We have a pool in the back. We have a pool and a pond. Pond would be good for you."

4. "If I woke up tomorrow with my head sewn to the carpet, I couldn't be more surprised."

5. "I don't even know your name."
   "Bend over!"
   "Ben? Nice to meet you."

6. "As Jean-Paul Sartre once said, 'How do you spell Sartre?' "

7. "Step out anyplace you want."
   "Any chance of stopping the car first? How 'bout slowing down to 55?"

Chevy Chase

1. National Lampoon's Vacation
   This scene takes place in a part of the country the Griswalds don't see very often, which Clark thinks is good until he hears a gunshot. Then what does he say?

2. Fletch
   What is Fletch's "smaller story"?

3. Caddyshack
   Ty Webb may be the best golfer at the club, but he's not the club champion. Who is?

4. National Lampoon's Christmas Vacation
   What does Clark receive as a Christmas bonus?

5. Fletch Lives
   What is the name of Fletch's estate?

6. Spies Like Us
   What actress plays Chase's love interest?

7. Seems Like Old Times
   Who wrote the screenplay?

ANSWERS TO BONUS QUESTIONS

1. "Roll 'em up."
2. Off Track Betting in the Himalayas
3. Dr. Beeper
4. a one-year membership in the Jelly-of-the-Month Club
5. Belle Isle
6. Donna Dixon
7. Neil Simon

Arnold Schwarzenegger

1. "You wouldn't hurt me, would you, sweetheart? Sweetheart, be reasonable, after all, we're married."
   "Consider this a divorce."

2. "It's not a tumor. It's not a tumor at all."

3. "I'll be back."

4. "Hey, lighthead, hey, Christmas tree."

5. "Come on. Come on, do it. Kill me, I'm here, kill me."

Arnold Schwarzenegger
1. Total Recall
   Which actress plays Arnold's wife?

2. Kindergarten Cop
   Who directed this movie?

3. The Terminator
   Although Arnold says this line in several movies, it was made famous in this movie. Who is the Terminator trying to terminate?

4. The Running Man
   When Arnold says "I'll be back" to Killian (Richard Dawson), how does Killian respond?

5. Predator
   True or false: Arnold kills the Predator.

ANSWERS TO BONUS QUESTIONS

1. Sharon Stone
2. Ivan Reitman
3. Sarah Connor (Linda Hamilton)
4. "Only in a rerun."
5. False: it destroys itself.

Woody Allen

1. "I ran a health food store in Greenwich Village. Occasionally a customer would get botulism. But that was very rare."

2. "Naturally, I, you know, the sudden appearance of a black spot on my back."
   "It was on your shirt."

3. "What is this the guy so upset about? You'd think nobody was ever compared to Mussolini before."

4. "I want to have three children."
   "Yes. One of each."

5. "La-di-da. La-di-da."

6. "I was so touched by her that, I don't know, after fifteen minutes I wanted to marry her, and after half an hour I completely gave up the idea of snatching her purse."

7. "This trial is a travesty. It's a travesty of a mockery of a sham of a mockery of a travesty of two mockerys of a sham."

8. "It was I who first said that clitoral orgasm should not be only for women. They laughed at me, ridiculed me. Said I was mad."

Woody Allen

1. Sleeper
   What car still ran, hundreds of years after it was made?

2. Hannah and Her Sisters
   According to Nietzsche, we live the same life over and over again exactly the same. What about this bothers Micky (Allen)?

3. Crimes and Misdemeanors
   When was the last time Cliff Stern (Allen) was inside a woman?

4. Love and Death
   What crime was Boris (Allen) executed for?

5. Annie Hall
   Where did Alvy Singer (Allen) live as a child?

6. Take the Money and Run
   What instrument does Virgil (Allen) play in the marching band?

7. Bananas
   What country does Fielding (Allen) become the president of?

8. Everything You Always Wanted to Know about Sex* (*but were afraid to ask)
   What animal does Gene Wilder fall in love with?

ANSWERS TO BONUS QUESTIONS

1. the Volkswagen Beetle
2. "That means I'll have to sit through the Ice Capades again."
3. "The last time I was inside a woman was when I visited the Statue of Liberty."
4. the attempted assassination of Napoléon
5. under the roller coaster at Coney Island
6. the cello
7. the Republic of San Marco
8. a sheep

Part Five

A QUOTER'S
Paradise for Experts

Repetition is the key to this section. Seeing a film only once will leave you short-handed as you negotiate these quotes. Only those who don't get out of the house enough dare proceed.

1. "I don't care how many of you dago, guinea, wop, greaseball goombas come out of the woodwork."
   "I'm German Irish."
   "Well, let me tell you something my kraut, mick friend."

2. "Do you know what time it is?"
   "Ten-fifteen."
   "Ten-fifteen? Try five after two!"
   "Why should I try five after two when it's ten-fifteen?"

3. "Let me explain. No, there is too much. Let me sum up."

4. "Hey, cowgirls. See the grass? Don't eat it."

5. "The popcorn you're eating has been pissed in. Film at eleven."

6. "Anyway, you can't scare her, she's sleeping with Prince Valium tonight."

7. "I thought he knew the guy, okay, Sam? I can't believe he didn't know the guy. . . . He does the merengue."

8. "Anything else that'll keep this elevator from falling?"
   "Yeah, the basement."

9. "Was she feelin' all right last night?"
   "She felt great to me."

10. "Be careful with the car, pal, it's a classic."

1. The Godfather
   Who wrote the 1969 book on which this film is based?

2. The Sunshine Boys
   According to Willie Clark (Walter Matthau), which words are funny?

3. The Princess Bride
   What will Inigo Montoya (Mandy Patinkin) do when he finds the six-fingered man he is searching for?

4. A League of Their Own
   What is the name of the team from Rockford that Lovitz is the scout for?

5. The Kentucky Fried Movie
   In case of premature ejaculation, the *Joy of Sex* tape is equipped with what?

6. Beetlejuice
   How do you summon Beetlejuice (Michael Keaton)?

7. Tin Men
   What actress plays the soon to be ex-wife of Tulley (Danny De-Vito)?

8. Speed
   What is the number of the bus with the bomb on it?

9. Fletch Lives
   Which of the following is not an alias used by Fletch (Chevy Chase)?
   a) Peggy Lee Zorba   b) Bobby Lee Swartz
   c) Henry Himmler   d) Elmer Fudd Gantry
   e) Claude Henry Smoot
   f) none of the above

10. Wise Guys
    Who directed this 1986 flick?

ANSWERS TO BONUS QUESTIONS

1. Mario Puzo
2. "Words with a 'K' are funny."
3. He will go up to the six-fingered man and say "Hello. My name is Inigo Montoya. You killed my father. Prepare to die."
4. the Peaches
5. Big Jim Slade, former tight end for the Kansas City Chiefs
6. You say his name three times.
7. Barbara Hershey
8. 2525
9. f) none of the above
10. Brian De Palma

11. "It happens sometimes. People just explode, natural causes."

12. "That picture on the wall back there. That wouldn't by any chance be Mussolini?"
    "It ain't Tony Bennett."

13. "And that's the double truth, Ruth."

14. "Santa, is there a back way out of this place?"
    "Of course there is, Lee, but this is one Santa that's going out the front door!"

15. "What's wrong with a kiss, boy? You don't have to go leaping straight for the clitoris like a bull at a gate."

16. "I'll get 'em anyway."
    "Why?"
    " 'Cause I don't know enough about killin' to kill him."

17. "Hanrahan. Suzanne sucks pussy."

18. "We've got bush!"

19. "Don't worry, this is going to be easy."
    "Not for me. I'm not an actor, I'm a movie star!"

20. "What's your name?"
    "Fuck you—that's my name."

11. Repo Man
    What actor plays the career repo man who shows Otto (Emilio Estevez) the ropes?

12. The Freshman
    Which actor plays the Mafia boss?

13. Do the Right Thing
    Which actor plays Sal, the owner of Sal's Pizzeria?

14. Scrooged
    Which actor plays the Ghost of Christmas Past?

15. Monty Python's The Meaning of Life
    What is the final item of food the obese man eats before he explodes?

16. The Sting
    According to Henry Gondorf (Paul Newman), who is revenge for?

17. Slap Shot
    What actor plays Reggie Dunlop, the team's captain?

18. Revenge of the Nerds
    Which actor plays Coach Harris?

19. My Favorite Year
    When Swann (Peter O'Toole) arrives drunk for his meeting with the TV executives, one of them says, "He's plastered." How does Swann respond?

20. Glengarry Glen Ross
    What two prizes have the agency owners added to this month's sales contest?

ANSWERS TO BONUS QUESTIONS

11. Harry Dean Stanton plays Bud in this 1983 cult film directed by Alex Cox.
12. Marlon Brando
13. Danny Aiello
14. David Johansen, aka Buster Poindexter
15. a wafer-thin mint
16. "Revenge is for suckers."
17. Paul Newman
18. John Goodman
19. "So are some of the finest erections in Europe."
20. "Second prize is a set of steak knives. Third prize is you're fired."

21. "Phone call from God? If it had been collect, it would have been daring."

22. "They oughta transfer you to Missing Persons, Streebek, you know everybody."

23. "It's economically unsound to grow up."

24. "What you got in there?"
"In here? Doom."

25. "Would you hold my wallet while I take the test, please? There's one thousand dollars in there. Or maybe there isn't. Know what I mean?"

26. "Nothing shocks me, I'm a scientist."

27. "Squeal like a pig. That's it, squeal."

28. "Well said, well spoken."

29. "You can read Dostoyevsky in the can."
"Yes, but you can't finish it."

30. "So my theory is that all the characters are Hamlet. I mean, it's all happening inside Hamlet's head so you only need one actor. Am I crazy?"

21. Dead Poets Society
Who wrote the introduction that Mr. Keating (Robin Williams) has the students rip out of their poetry textbooks?

22. Dragnet
What relation is Joe Friday (Dan Aykroyd) to the original Joe Friday?

23. Nothing in Common
What is the last line Mr. Basner (Jackie Gleason) says to his son?

24. The Color of Money
What character does Paul Newman play?

25. Spies Like Us
"If you're discovered appropriating classified documents at a foreign consulate reception you should? a) express concern b) act surprised c) deny everything d) all three."

26. Indiana Jones and The Temple of Doom
What is the name of the club where the movie opens?

27. Deliverance
Who are the four actors who go canoeing?

28. Seems Like Old Times
What crime is Nick (Chevy Chase) wanted for?

29. The Big Chill
What college did all the main characters attend together?

30. Soapdish
What show is Jeffrey Anderson (Kevin Kline) doing when David Barnes (Robert Downey, Jr.) finds him?

ANSWERS TO BONUS QUESTIONS

21. J. Evans Pritchart, Ph.D.
22. He's his nephew.
23. "You're the last person I ever thought would come through for me."
24. the pool shark, Fast Eddie Felson
25. d) all three
26. the Club Obi Wan

27. Jon Voight, Burt Reynolds, Ned Beatty, and Ronny Cox
28. robbing a bank
29. University of Michigan
30. a retirement home dinner theater production of *Death of a Salesman*

31. "It's not the voltage that gets you, it's the amps."

32. "Fluff 'n' Fold, buddy. As soon as I make it really big, I'm going Fluff 'n' Fold."

33. "Whaddya doin'? That guy's the biggest cunt-hound in Bay Ridge."

34. "Was it hard for you in the Resistance?"
"Very hard, but not as hard as it is now."

35. "What you see is a guy who never measured a man's success by the size of his wallet!"

36. "Get your ass to Mars."

37. "Pretty good, huh? You can't spell it, but it eats pretty good."

38. "The sexual revolution is over, everybody out of bed."

39. "She got that magna cum laude pussy on her that done fried up your brain."

40. "What kind of a host invites you to his house for the weekend and dies on you?"

41. "Under the circumstances she would have said anything. She would have fucked a snake."

31. Running Scared
What does Ray (Gregory Hines) have to do to prove to the lawyer that he's a "paisan"?

32. St. Elmo's Fire
From what school did all the main characters just graduate?

33. Saturday Night Fever
What is the name of the dance club where the gang hangs out?

34. The Pink Panther Strikes Again
This is the fourth time Peter Sellers portrays Inspector Clouseau. What are the previous three Clouseau movies?

35. Wall Street
What is the name of Mr. Fox's (Martin Sheen) airline?

36. Total Recall
Who is the leader of the mutants?

37. The Natural
For what team does Roy Hobbs (Robert Redford) play?

38. The Secret of My Success
What actress plays Brantley's (Michael J. Fox) love interest?

39. Basic Instinct
What is the name of Ms. Tramell's (Sharon Stone) plot-similar book?

40. Weekend at Bernie's
Name the two actors who play the star living characters in this flick.

41. Tequila Sunrise
Which actress plays the object of everyone's affections?

ANSWERS TO BONUS QUESTIONS

31. "What do you want me to do? Cook you up a pot of ragu? Sweat garlic? Sing an opera, lose a war?"
32. Georgetown University
33. 2001 Odyssey Club
34. *The Pink Panther* (1964), *A Shot in the Dark* (1964), and *The Return of the Pink Panther* (1975)
35. Bluestar
36. Kwato
37. the New York Knights
38. Helen Slater
39. *Love Hurts*
40. Jonathan Silverman and Andrew McCarthy
41. Michelle Pfeiffer

42. "Hey, well, that's cool, baby. I mean, you know how it is—rockin' and rollin' and what not."

43. "I'm sailing. I sail. I'm a sailor."

44. "Know your limitations. You are a moron."

45. "What kind of clown are you?"
"The crying on the inside kind, I guess."

46. "I'd like to make her look a little more attractive. How far can you pull back?"
"How do you feel about Cleveland?"

47. "Bonanza is not an accurate description of the Old West. . . . It's a fifty-year-old father with three forty-seven-year-old sons. You know why they get along good, 'cause they're all the same age."

48. "Why do they call her Lassie?"

49. "They mostly come out at night. Mostly."

50. "She'll wrap her legs around you so tight you'll be beggin' for mercy."
"Well, I'll stay away from her, then."

51. "You never saw a guy who slept with a fish before?"

52. "Oh, excuse me, sir. I lost my ID in a flood and I was wondering, would you pick me up some Old Harper's hard stuff?"
"Why certainly. I lost my wife, too. Her name wasn't ID, though and it wasn't in a flood."

53. "He's yellin', 'Nail her, nail her.' I look in the rearview, the guy's havin' some kind of asthma attack. Turns out he's yellin' 'Inhaler, inhaler.' "

42. Grease
What high school do the characters attend?

43. What about Bob?
What is the name of Dr. Marvin's (Richard Dreyfuss) book?

44. Dirty Rotten Scoundrels
Name the two actors who play the con men.

45. Quick Change
Who plays this clown?

46. Tootsie
What is the name of Dustin Hoffman's character as a man, and what is it as a woman?

47. Tin Men
Where did Lou find God?

48. Porky's
What is Porky's?

49. Aliens
What kind of poontang is the best poontang, according to the Marines?

50. Big
What New York City toy store is the site of the giant piano?

51. Splash
True or false: Alan (Tom Hanks) decides to become a merman at the end?

52. American Graffiti
What DJ is on the radio throughout the movie?

53. Casual Sex?
What character does Andrew Dice Clay play?

ANSWERS TO BONUS QUESTIONS

42. Rydell High
43. *Baby Steps*
44. Michael Caine and Steve Martin
45. Bill Murray
46. Michael Dorsey and Dorothy Michaels
47. at the smorgasbord
48. It's a bar and brothel.

49. Arturian poontang
50. F.A.O. Schwartz
51. true
52. Wolfman Jack
53. "I'm the best from the east, I'm a wild crazy beast, I'm the Vin man."

54. "These men have taken a supreme vow of celibacy, like their fathers, and their fathers before them."

55. "I've seen the future. It's a bald-headed man from New York."

56. "The upside-down fan is Phil Brody."

57. "Why you pull a knife? I ain't be gotten no weapon."

58. "Five, four, three, two, one. Let 'er fly. In and out."

59. "And if you do . . . And if you do . . ."

60. "We miss the bus, they miss the bus, when's the next bus? Summa cum laude, magna cum laude, the radio's too loudy."

61. "Would you say I have a plethora of pinatas?"

62. "Because there is a heart here that wants you to know—that there's a possible five-oh-two on Main, proceed to Main."

63. "Everything you're doing is bad, I want you to know this."

64. "Turbulence. Solar radiation heats the earth's crust, warm air rises, cool air descends—turbulence. I don't like that."

54. Hot Shots!: Part Deux
What actress plays Topper's (Charlie Sheen) love interest?

55. Lost in America
Which actor plays the casino manager?

56. The Flamingo Kid
Which actor plays Phil Brody?

57. Hollywood Shuffle
According to Tyrone, the movie critic, how could Chicago Jones jump off a mountain and not hurt himself?

58. Hoosiers
What school does Hickory play in the state finals?

59. Good Morning, Vietnam
What DJ follows "The Adrian Cronhour"?

60. Johnny Dangerously
What actor plays the district attorney?

61. ¡Three Amigos!
Name the three actors who play the Amigos?

62. Roxanne
Who wrote the play *Cyrano de Bergerac,* on which this film is loosely based?

63. Ghostbusters II
Where is Yanosh from?

64. The Hunt for Red October
What does Ramius (Sean Connery) think the chances are for him and his officers to defect?

ANSWERS TO BONUS QUESTIONS

54. Valeria Golino
55. Garry Marshall
56. Richard Crenna
57. "Because he did brace himself. And he knew something about the levels of gravitivity and polarity."
58. South Bend Central
59. Dan "the Man" Levitan
60. Danny DeVito
61. Chevy Chase, Steve Martin, and Martin Short
62. Edmond Rostand
63. the Upper West Side
64. one chance in three

65. "My bitch better have my money, through rain sleet, or snow."

66. "John Wayne was a fag."

67. "I had fried food for lunch again today. I know, I know, I shouldn't've had it, but I couldn't help myself. Do you think I lack self-discipline?"

68. "You cannot have the duck. Do you think with a financial statement like this you can have the duck?"

69. "I got an urge tonight to, I don't know, go out tonight and—stomp some ass!"

70. "It's a great tradition. They throw a great party for you on the one day you can't come."

71. "I'm just standing up for my rights—as a consumer."

72. "Besides, I wanna try this thing. . . . It's good for the lats, good for the pecks."

73. "Look at this, combination hookah and coffeemaker, also makes chili and fries."

74. "So, what do you think? Women. A mistake? Or did He do it to us on purpose?"

75. "Your best friend is your dick."
"And where did I learn that from? Your best friend is your dick."
"That's great. The four of us will go out for lunch someday."

65. I'm Gonna Git You, Sucka
This is the first line of a poem for which Fly Guy wins an award. Name the award.

66. Repo Man
What is Miller the mechanic's theory about the correlation between driving and intelligence?

67. The Sure Thing
What does Gib (John Cusack) order for this large man to drink?

68. L.A. Story
Harris (Steve Martin) is trying to get a reservation at what restaurant?

69. The Wanderers
What is the name of the Asian gang?

70. The Big Chill
What is the ultimate act of self-absorption, according to Nick (William Hurt)?

71. Falling Down
Where is Bill Foster (Michael Douglas) trying to get?

72. Club Paradise
What is Barry (Rick Moranis) trying?

73. Aladdin
Who is the voice of the Genie?

74. The Witches of Eastwick
What character does Jack Nicholson play?

75. Nothing in Common
David Basner (Tom Hanks) is doing the ad campaign for what airline?

ANSWERS TO BONUS QUESTIONS

65. Pimp of the Year
66. "The more you drive, the less intelligent you are."
67. a trough of spritzer
68. L'Idiot
69. the Wongs
70. masturbation
71. to his ex-wife's house for his daughter's birthday
72. windsurfing
73. Robin Williams
74. Daryl Van Horne
75. Colonial Air Lines

76. "Come on, Charlie, you got to admit she looks like she could fuck you right in half, I mean, just fuck you to pieces."

77. "You will cream in your jeans when you see *Catholic High School Girls in Trouble*."

78. "I just go out and just play basketball. Good, hard-nosed basketball. Things happen throughout the course of the game, there's nothing you can do."
"Anything else?"
"Yes. Steve, don't come yet."

79. "Who loves you and who do you love?"

80. "Please sir, if you don't get back in line . . ."
". . . Then what? I'll be arrested? Put in airport jail? Just get your ticket and move on. Get your goddamn ticket and move on!"

81. "Not playing to win is like sleeping with your sister. Sure, she's a great piece of tail with a blouse full of goodies, but it's just illegal."

82. "This is for ladies only."
"As is this, Madam, but every now and again I have to run a little water through it."

83. "You know, I heard you had balls big enough to come in a dump truck, but you don't look like much to me."
"Opinions vary."

84. "Myron T. Spargo, plumbing contractor. Myron was impudent . . . Imagine that, man lays pipe for a living, can't get it up at home."

85. "Okay, okay, what movie? 'Well, this was not a boating accident.' "

86. "There's no reason to shoot at me, I'm a dentist."

76. Something Wild
    What actress plays this wild woman?

77. The Kentucky Fried Movie
    What is the title of the film that spoofs *Enter the Dragon?*

78. Singles
    What hoopster is Steve thinking of during sex?

79. The Running Man
    What real-life game show host plays Damon Killian?

80. Honeymoon in Vegas
    Who does Jack (Nicholas Cage) catch a flight to Las Vegas with?

81. Hot Shots!
    Continuing the same monologue, what kind of kids do you get then?

82. My Favorite Year
    Which two celebrities, if brought to her house, can Benjy's ma call "Al"?

83. Road House
    What actor plays the villain Brad Wesley?

84. Dead Again
    What actor says these lines?

85. Stakeout
    In this scene, Chris (Richard Dreyfuss) and Bill (Emilio Estevez) are playing their own version of What's That From? What movie is the line from?

86. The In-Laws
    What evasive tactic does Vince (Peter Falk) give Sheldon (Alan Arkin) to avoid being shot?

ANSWERS TO BONUS QUESTIONS

76. Melanie Griffith
77. *A Fistful of Yen*
78. Xavier McDaniel
79. Richard Dawson
80. the Flying Elvises, Utah chapter
81. "Then you get . . . kids with no teeth who only play the banjo, drink applesauce through a straw, poke farm animals."
82. Al Capone and Al Jolson
83. Ben Gazzara
84. Robin Williams
85. Richard Dreyfuss says it in *Jaws.*
86. "Serpentine, serpentine."

87. "If this is foreplay, I'm a dead man."

88. "Having fun, sweetie?"
"I sure am, because I just dropped two crab cakes in my shorts and nobody knows."

89. "Did you get in her pants?"
"She's not that kind of a girl."
"Why? She have a penis?"

90. "Doesn't Lucky Chucky want to come out? Your love machine, your throbbing thrill hammer, your thing?"

91. "If you win twenty in the show, you can let the fungus grow back on your shoes and the press will think you're colorful."

92. "This is not 'good-bye', it's just 'I won't ever see you again.' "

87. Cocoon
    Who directed this flick?

88. Mr. Saturday Night
    What is the name of the comedian Billy Crystal plays?

89. Revenge of the Nerds
    What is the sister sorority of the Tri Lambdas?

90. Peggy Sue Got Married
    Who directed this movie?

91. Bull Durham
    How many minor league home runs does Crash (Kevin Costner) hit in his career?

92. Naked Gun 33 1/3: The Final Insult
    At what event does the climax of the film take place?

ANSWERS TO BONUS QUESTIONS

87. Ron Howard
88. Buddy Young, Jr.
89. the Omega Moos

90. Francis Ford Coppola
91. 247
92. at the Academy Awards

Part Six

Classic Quotes
by Category

The National Pastime

As long as there has been baseball, there have been stories about baseball. In recent decades, these stories have been not just about hitting the game-winning home run in the big game, but also about making us laugh and cry in the process. Can you identify these lines from baseball movies?

1. "Are you crying? There's no crying. There's no crying in baseball."

2. "We got a game with the Athletics Wednesday and that means only one thing—bad news for the Athletics."

3. "When I walk down the street, people will look at me and say 'There goes Roy Hobbes. The best there ever was.' "

4. "Is this heaven?"
   "No. It's Iowa."

5. "What the hell league you been playin' in?"
   "California Penal."

6. "My Triple A contract gets bought out so I can hold the Flavor of the Month stick in the bus leagues, is that it? Well fuck this fucking game."

7. "These guys don't look so tough."
   "Yeah, that's what Custer said when the Indians took the field."

8. "It's the Eliminator. I got a new one I'll show you. You get a piece of it, I'll let you name it."
   "I'll call it the Masturbator."

1. A League of Their Own
   Who directed this movie?

2. The Bad News Bears
   What business sponsors the Bears?

3. The Natural
   What is the name of Roy's (Redford) bat?

4. Field of Dreams
   Who lives in Chisholm, Minnesota?

5. Major League
   What character does Wesley Snipes play, and how does he identify himself?

6. Bull Durham
   According to Annie (Susan Sarandon), what group of people
   passed on the tradition of breathing through your eyelids?

7. Eight Men Out
   When the manager Kid Gleason (John Mahoney) is put on the
   stand to testify against his players, he's asked, "What do you think
   of your players now?" What does he say?

8. Major League II
   What actor plays the die-hard, disappointed fan who sings, "Wild
   Thing, you make my butt sting. I detest you."

ANSWERS TO BONUS QUESTIONS

1. Penny Marshall
2. Chico's Bail Bonds
3. Wonderboy
4. Archibald "Moonlight" Graham (Burt Lancaster)
5. "Willie Mays Hayes. Plays like Mays, but I run like Hayes."
6. the Aztecs
7. "I think they're the greatest ball club I ever seen. Period."
8. Randy Quaid

Quoting at the O.K. Corral

John Wayne may have hung up his gun belt, but the Western still roams the movie set. Nowadays, the bad guys don't always wear black hats, and the hero doesn't always ride off into the sunset with Grace Kelly, but the lines are still memorable.

1. "I can't swim!"
   "Why you crazy? The fall will probably kill ya."

2. "You're so drunk . . . you're probably seeing double."
   "I got two guns, one for each of ya."

3. "Regulators! Let's saddle up."

4. "I was just ropin' over there, thought I'd mosey on over. I never moseyed before, I hope I did it right."

5. "Badges? We don't need no stinkin' badges."

6. "It's a hell of a thing, killing a man. Take away all he's got and all he's ever gonna have."

7. "I'll make ya famous."

1. Butch Cassidy and the Sundance Kid
   What is the name of Butch's (Newman) gang?

2. Tombstone
   In what state was Wyatt Earp (Kurt Russell) a lawman?

3. Young Guns
   What is Billy the Kid's (Emilio Estevez) real name?

4. City Slickers
   When Bonnie (Helen Slater) says "Good night," Ed (Bruno Kirby) thinks it really means something else. What?

5. Blazing Saddles
   This line is actually a spoof of a similar line from a different movie. Which one?

6. Unforgiven
   How much is the reward offered by the whores?

7. Young Guns II
   Name the real-life character who claimed to be Billy the Kid.

ANSWERS TO BONUS QUESTIONS

1. the Hole in the Wall Gang
2. Kansas
3. William H. Bonney
4. "I like your ass, could I wear it as a hat?"
5. *The Treasure of Sierra Madre*
6. $1,000
7. Brushy Bill Roberts

Till Death Do Us Part

Nothing speaks volumes quite like deep, heartfelt love. It stirs in us a desire for words echoing Shakespeare and Byron. Of course, men and women in love don't always have the kindest words for each other.

1. "I'm in love with you."
   "Snap out of it!"

2. "How long do you like to be held afterwards? All night, right? See, that's the problem. Somewhere between thirty seconds and all night is your problem."
   "I don't have a problem."
   "Yes you do."

3. "Life is pain, Highness. Anyone who says differently is selling something."

4. "You stick out like a sore thumb around here."
   "Oh yeah, you blend."

5. "Why do you think I'm a lawyer?"
   "You've got that sharp, useless look about you."

6. "I'm not gonna hurt ya, I'm just gonna bash your brains in."

7. "Oh Kent, we were only hurting each other."
   "I thought that was the way you wanted it."

8. "You got a look in your eye like you ain't been fucked in a year."

9. "You never ask me what's on the flip side."
   "No, because I don't give a shit. Who cares about what's on the flip side of a record?"

1. Moonstruck
How did Ronny (Nicholas Cage) lose his hand?

2. When Harry Met Sally . . .
Harry (Billy Crystal) says a man can never be just friends with a woman he finds attractive, because he wants to have sex with her. But what does he say about women he finds unattractive?

3. The Princess Bride
Who kidnapped Westley (Cary Elwes)?

4. My Cousin Vinny
Which actress won an Oscar for her work in this film?

5. Pretty Woman
When asked how she enjoyed the opera, Vivian (Julia Roberts) blurts out "It was so good I almost peed my pants." How does Edward (Richard Gere) rephrase her response?

6. The Shining
What is the name of the hotel?

7. Hot Shots!
What two NBA All-Stars appear in this flick?

8. Scarface
Who wrote this screenplay?

9. Diner
What's on the flip side of "Good Golly Miss Molly"?

ANSWERS TO BONUS QUESTIONS

1. He caught it in a bread slicer.
2. "Nah, you pretty much wanna nail them too."
3. the Dread Pirate Roberts
4. Marisa Tomei won for Best Supporting Actress in 1992.
5. "She said she liked it better than *The Pirates of Penzance.*"
6. the Overlook Hotel
7. Bill Laimbeer and Charles Barkley
8. Oliver Stone
9. "Hey Hey, Hey Hey"

10. "Get out of my life!"
    "Wait one minute. This is my life, you get out!"
    "I'm going nowhere, babe. Get used to it."

11. "Please don't justify yourself, it's pathetic. If you tell me to fuck off,
    I'd have more respect for you."
    "All right then, fuck off."

12. "I'd just as soon kiss a wookie."
    "I can arrange that."

13. "Say something romantic."
    "You, you have a great body. Your knockers, your, no, not your knock-
    ers, your breasts. Your breasts are like melons. Not melons, like pillows.
    Could I, can I fluff your pillows?"

10. Soapdish
Why don't actors like to play people in comas, according to David (Robert Downey, Jr.)?

11. Fatal Attraction
What does Alex (Glenn Close) do with Dan's (Michael Douglas) daughter's pet rabbit?

12. The Empire Strikes Back
What animal does Han Solo (Harrison Ford) put Luke (Mark Hamill) in to keep him from freezing to death at the beginning of the film?

13. Roxanne
This movie is based on what play?

ANSWERS TO BONUS QUESTIONS

10. "Actors don't like to play comas, they feel it limits the range."
11. She boils it.
12. a Ton Ton
13. *Cyrano de Bergerac*

You Have the Right to Remain Silent

Almost all movie cops read someone his or her rights at least once, but they don't always follow the book. Which movies featured these variations on the Miranda warning?

1. "You have the right to have to a court appointed attorney. You have a right to sing the blues. You have the right to cable TV, that's very important. You have the right to sublet. You have the right to paint the walls, no loud colors."

2. "You have the right to an attorney. You have the right to a continental breakfast. You have the right to the beverage of your choice in the precinct coffee shop."

3. "You have the right to remain unconscious. Anything you say ain't gonna be much."

4. "You have the right to remain silent. You have the right to have your face kicked in by me. You have the right to have your balls stomped by him."

1. Police Academy 2: Their First Assignment
   What actor says these lines?

2. Running Scared
   What actor plays Julio Gonzalez?

3. Lethal Weapon 3
   At what sporting event does Leo Getz (Joe Pesci) get shot?

4. Fletch
   What is Fletch's (Chevy Chase) byline?

ANSWERS TO BONUS QUESTIONS

1. Steve Guttenberg
2. Jimmy Smits

3. a Los Angeles Kings hockey game
4. Jane Doe

Give Him a Pair of Concrete Shoes

Mobsters kill, extort, and rob, but we love them anyway, especially when they are larger than life on the big screen. The old days had Humphrey Bogart and James Cagney, but I grew up on one image of the gangster: Marlon Brando as Don Vito Corleone. He was indeed the Godfather, for he inspired many a thug, and many a line from gangster movies that followed.

1. "Sonny had five fingers, but he only used three."

2. "He taught me, 'Keep your friends close, but your enemies closer.' "

3. "I'm gonna get the papers, get the papers."

4. "Fuck you and your family. You got nothing . . . and if you were a man, you woulda done it by now."

5. "You shouldn't hang me on a hook. My father hung me on a hook once. Once."

6. "I'm gonna make him an offer he can't refuse."

7. "Have another cookie, my dear?"

1. A Bronx Tale
   Who wrote this screenplay?

2. The Godfather Part II
   What has history taught us, if it has taught us anything, according to Michael (Al Pacino)?

3. GoodFellas
   Which character says this line?

4. The Untouchables
   According to Capone (De Niro), how do you know who has won a prize fight?

5. Johnny Dangerously
   What actor plays the leader of the Dundee gang?

6. The Godfather
   True or false: Francis Ford Coppola won the Best Director Oscar for this film.

7. Prizzi's Honor
   What actress played Mayrose Prizzi?

ANSWERS TO BONUS QUESTIONS

1. Chazz Palmenteri
2. "If anything in this life is certain, if history has taught us anything, it's that you can kill anyone."
3. Jimmy Two Times
4. "You got an all-out prize fight, you wait till the fight's over, one guy's left standing and that's how you know who won."
5. Peter Boyle
6. False. He won it for *The Godfather Part II*.
7. Anjelica Huston won the Best Supporting Actress Oscar for her performance in 1985.

Sing about It

Sometimes thoughts are best expressed not in dialogue, but in song. All of the following quotes are meant to be sung out loud, only then can their full meaning (and the comedy therein) be brought out.

1. "Tonight is your night, bro.
Tonight is your night, bro!"

2. "I can sing while I read,
I am singing—and reading—both!"

3. "Rollin', rollin', rollin',
Keep them doggies rollin',
Man my ass is swollen—Rawhide!

4. "I'm picking out a thermos for you.
Not an ordinary thermos for you."

5. "Strangers in the night,
Exchanging clothing. . . .
Strangers in my pants . . ."

6. "She may get wooly.
Young girls, they do get wooly . . ."

7. "I was born to love you,
I was born to lick your face."

8. "The Desert Inn has heart.
The Desert Inn has heart."

9. "Viva Danang, Oh Viva Danang.
Danang me, Danang me,
Why don't they get a rope and hang me?"

ANSWERS AND BONUS QUESTIONS

1. Twins
   Where is the island that Julius (Arnold Shwarzenegger) is from?

2. Broadcast News
   According to Aaron (Albert Brooks), what is an ass kisser?

3. City Slickers
   What does Mitch (Billy Crystal) do for a living?

4. The Jerk
   When Navin (Steve Martin) leaves home, his father gives him two rules to follow. What are they?

5. Fletch
   Does Fletch (Chevy Chase) own rubber gloves?

6. Bull Durham
   Annie (Susan Sarandon) is sure that Nuke (Tim Robbins) will do fine, because the world was made for the type of person he is. What type is this?

7. Caddyshack
   What are two things Lacy Underalls says she likes to do for fun?

8. Lost in America
   What number does Linda (Julie Hagerty) keep betting on to win back the nest egg?

9. Good Morning, Vietnam
   "What does three up and three down mean to you, airman?"

ANSWERS TO BONUS QUESTIONS

1. "Three hundred nautical miles south-southwest of Fiji."
2. "I think anyone who puckers up their lips and presses it against their boss's buttocks and then smooches is an ass kisser."
3. He sells advertising time on a radio station.
4. "1) The Lord loves a hardworking man. 2) Never trust whitey."
5. No. He rents them.
6. "The world was made for people who aren't cursed with self-awareness."
7. "Skinny-skiing. Going to bullfights on acid."
8. twenty-two
9. "End of an inning?"

138   CLASSIC QUOTES BY CATEGORY

And God Created Woman

Since the days of Mae West and Bette Davis, women have always had some of the snappiest lines in movies. Here are a few of the more memorable lines by leading ladies of recent decades.

1. "I am Catwoman, hear me roar."

2. "Hey, Goose, you big stud! Take me to bed or lose me forever."

3. "You're not too smart, are you? I like that in a man."

4. "I'm not going to be ignored, Dan."

5. "In time you will see that this is the best thing."
   "In time you'll drop dead and I'll come to your funeral in a red dress."

6. "I've got a head for business and a bod for sin. Is there anything wrong with that?"

7. "Would somebody get this big walking carpet out of my way?"

8. "And I'm gonna be forty."
   "When?"
   "Someday."

9. "You know your last name's an adverb?"

10. "Of course, a guy'll listen to anything if he thinks it's foreplay."

11. "Oh, Bob. Do I have any openings that this man might fit?"

1. Batman Returns
   What is Catwoman's (Michelle Pfeiffer) real name?

2. Top Gun
   Who plays Goose?

3. Body Heat
   What actor plays Matty's (Kathleen Turner) husband?

4. Fatal Attraction
   What actress plays Dan's (Michael Douglas) wife?

5. Moonstruck
   What is the name of Loretta's (Cher) father and what actor plays him?

6. Working Girl
   Who directed this film?

7. Star Wars
   What character is nicknamed the "walking carpet"?

8. When Harry Met Sally . . .
   What actress plays Sally's (Meg Ryan) friend Marie?

9. Johnny Dangerously
   What disease is abbreviated E.S.S?

10. Bull Durham
    Nuke (Tim Robbins) set five new league records in his professional debut. Can you name them?

11. History of the World Part One
    What part of Ethiopia does Josephus say he's from?

ANSWERS TO BONUS QUESTIONS

1. Salina Kane
2. Anthony Edwards
3. Richard Crenna
4. Anne Archer
5. Cosmo, played by Vincent Gardenia
6. Mike Nichols
7. Chewbacca the Wookie

8. Carrie Fisher
9. Enlarged Scrotum Syndrome
10. 1) walked eighteen 2) struck out eighteen 3) hit the sportswriter 4) hit the PA announcer 5) hit the mascot twice
11. "One-hundred Twenty-fifth Street."

12. "Where's my Dicky? Oh, sorry."

13. "Nice beaver."
    "Thanks, I just had it stuffed."

14. "Close is a lingerie shop without a front window."

15. "I thought you were good, Paul, but you're not good. You're just another dirty birdy and I don't think I better be around you for a while."

16. "Listen, I appreciate this whole seduction scene you got going, but let me give you a tip—I'm a sure thing."

17. "I'm being marked down? What is this, the bargain basement? I've been kidnapped by Kmart."

18. "I'm goin', I'm goin'. I got the metal to the pedal and the thing to the floor."

19. "I'm not bad, I'm just drawn that way."

20. "Apes don't read philosophy."
    "Yes they do, Otto, they just don't understand it."

21. "She's a woman, Ernest, a woman. From Newark, for God's sake!"

22. "Fuck me gently with a chainsaw."

12. Murder by Death
    Why didn't Sam (Peter Falk) tell Angel (Eileen Brennan) that they needed oil before he sent her for the gas?

13. The Naked Gun: From the Files of Police Squad!
    According to Frank (Leslie Nielsen), what happens when you eat a spoonful of Draino?

14. Lethal Weapon 3
    What actress plays Lorna Koe?

15. Misery
    How did Misery die?

16. Pretty Woman
    What actor plays the hotel concierge?

17. Ruthless People
    Which two actors play the kidnappers?

18. Smokey and the Bandit
    What character does Jackie Gleason play in this 1977 movie?

19. Who Framed Roger Rabbit
    Who is the voice of Jessica Rabbit?

20. A Fish Called Wanda
    What does Archie (John Cleese) do for a living?

21. Death Becomes Her
    What two actresses play the women in Ernest's (Bruce Willis) life?

22. Heathers
    What actress plays the lead part in this movie?

ANSWERS TO BONUS QUESTIONS

12. "I gave you a fifty-dollar bill and the gas was only five bucks. Maybe you come back, maybe you wouldn't, I couldn't take that chance."
13. "It'll clean you out, but it'll leave you hollow inside."
14. Rene Russo.
15. She died in childbirth.
16. Hector Elizondo
17. Judge Reinhold and Helen Slater
18. Sheriff Buford T. Justice
19. Kathleen Turner
20. He's a barrister.
21. Meryl Streep and Goldie Hawn
22. Winona Ryder

Uncle Sam Wants You

Ever since Abbott and Costello joined up, the army has been not only a place of military training, but also a stamping ground for comedy and drama alike. All of the following lines are standard U.S military-movie issue. Ten hut!

1. "It was my fifth minute in the army and so far, I hated everyone."

2. "It's oh-six hundred. What's the 'oh' stand for? Oh my God, it's early."

3. "I feel the need—The need for speed."

4. "Charlie don't surf!"

5. "Name's Pete Thompson, but, uh, everybody calls me Dead Meat."

6. "That's the fact, Jack!"

1. Biloxi Blues
   Jerome (Matthew Broderick) thinks his army food looks familiar. Where does he say he's seen it before?

2. Good Morning, Vietnam
   Joey, the gay bar owner, wants naked photos of which American actor?

3. Top Gun
   What actress plays Goose's wife, Carol?

4. Apocalypse Now
   Upon what book is this based?

5. Hot Shots!
   How many times does a Chihuahua appear in the movie?

6. Stripes
   What is the name of John's (Bill Murray) drill sergeant?

ANSWERS TO BONUS QUESTIONS

1. At the Bronx Zoo: "The gorillas were throwing it at each other."
2. Walter Brennan
3. Meg Ryan
4. Joseph Conrad's *Heart of Darkness*
5. four
6. Sergeant Hawker

The Sequel

"If it ain't broke, don't fix it" is a proverb followed religiously by Hollywood. When a movie works, you can bet a sequel is not far behind. Despite their lack of originality, these sequels are sometimes quite good, and quite quotable.

1. "What did you say your name was?"
   "Nostradamus."
   "Nostra Damus? I love the Fightin' Irish."

2. "I don't think it's fair to call my clients frauds 'cause one time I turned into a dog and they helped me."

3. "Jimmy, do you like it when Scraps holds onto your leg and rubs up and down?"

4. "Whatever you need—Leo Getz. Get it?"

5. "He is just one, where you are three, or four, if you count him twice."

6. "Is this some kind of bust?"
   "Well, it's very impressive, yes. But we need to ask you a few questions."

7. "I can handle things. I'm smart, not like everybody says, like dumb, I'm smart and I want respect."

8. "I can't believe you two are from the same gene pool."
   "He's from the shallow end."

1. Fletch Lives
   What kind of watch does Fletch (Chevy Chase) have?

2. Ghostbusters II
   What is the museum security guard's favorite TV show?

3. Airplane II: The Sequel
   Which actor plays the man with the bomb?

4. Lethal Weapon 2
   Why does Leo (Joe Pesci) say he hates the Drive-Thru?

5. Superman II
   Where were the three prisoners from Krypton imprisoned?

6. Naked Gun 2½: The Smell of Fear
   What is Frank's (Leslie Nielsen) theory about betting on boxing?

7. The Godfather Part II
   What actor played Vito Corleone as a young man?

8. City Slickers II: The Legend of Curly's Gold
   What movies is Glen (Jon Lovitz) always quoting from?

ANSWERS TO BONUS QUESTIONS

1. a Championship Laker watch
2. *Bassmasters*
3. Sonny Bono
4. "They fuck you at the Drive-Thru."
5. the Phantom Zone
6. "All I know is never bet on the white guy."
7. Robert De Niro, who won the Best Supporting Actor Oscar for his performance
8. the *Godfather* movies

9. "That ball wouldn't have been out of a lot of parks."
   "Name one."
   "Yellowstone."

10. "Just the fax, ma'am. Just the fax."

11. "It's hot. It's like Africa hot. Tarzan couldn't take this kinda hot."

12. "Get yo mad ass in this pool with me."

13. "I shall finish the game, Doc."

14. "Never tell me the odds."

15. "Stop your grinnin' and drop your linen."

16. "You said there weren't gonna be a rematch."

17. "Fortune and glory kid, fortune and glory."

9. Major League II
   True or false: This line was also in the original movie.

10. Die Hard 2
    At what airport does this adventure take place?

11. Biloxi Blues
    What is Eugene's (Matthew Broderick) full name?

12. Beverly Hills Cop II
    After Taggert (John Ashton) says, "Technically, this is traffic duty," how does Chief Lutz respond?

13. Young Guns II
    Out of the original gang of Regulators, who are the only three to make it to the sequel?

14. The Empire Strikes Back
    Who is the voice of Darth Vader?

15. Aliens
    True or false: Ripley (Sigourney Weaver) is the only survivor of the first movie.

16. Rocky II
    When a reporter asks Rocky what he was thinking going into the last round of his first fight with Apollo (Carl Weathers), what does he say?

17. Indiana Jones and the Temple of Doom
    What goddess does the Thugee cult worship?

ANSWERS TO BONUS QUESTIONS

9. False. It was used in the trailers, but cut from the movie.
10. Dulles Airport in Washington, DC
11. Eugene Morris Jerome
12. "Technically, you're a goddamn idiot."
13. Billy the Kid (Emilio Estevez), Chavez (Lou Diamond Phillips), and Doc (Kiefer Sutherland)
14. James Earl Jones
15. true
16. "I don't know, that I should've stayed in school or something."
17. Kali

You Come Here Often?

The pickup line—it's too bad we can't think up these beauties on our own when we need them. Feel free to use them from now on, although I do not guarantee success. If you're lucky, you might get "What's that from?" instead of a slap in response.

1. "Hey vodka rocks. Whaddya say you and me get nipple to nipple?"
   "I can do that without you."

2. "You so fine, baby, I drink a tub of your bathwater."

3. "I'm a professional boxer. You know much about the fight game?"
   "No."
   "I'm the heavyweight champion of the world."

4. "Hey, Red, whaddya say, wanna join us for a colada?"
   "Frankly, I'd rather be drawn and quartered."
   "Oooh, kinky. Drawn and quartered? I think we're gonna need two other guys."

5. "If there's ever anything I can do for you, or more to the point, *to* you, all you need to do is ask, Okay?"
   "Can you hammer a six-inch spike into a board with your penis?"

6. "How would you like to have a sexual encounter so intense it could conceivably change your political views?"

1. Road House
   What is the name of the bar that Dalton (Patrick Swayze) is hired to clean up?

2. She's Gotta Have It
   What character does Spike Lee play?

3. About Last Night
   On what one-act play is this movie based?

4. Club Paradise
   What was Jack's (Robin Williams) job and in what city did he work before he moved to the island?

5. Real Genius
   What actor was just shot down thus?

6. The Sure Thing
   What actor plays Gary Cooper, the husband of the couple giving Gib (John Cusack) and Alison (Daphne Zuniga) a lift to California (before he throws them out of the car)?

ANSWERS TO BONUS QUESTIONS

1. the Double Deuce
2. Mars Blackmon
3. David Mamet's "Sexual Perversity in Chicago"
4. a Chicago fireman
5. Val Kilmer
6. Tim Robbins

Bad Guys Wear Black Hats

Not all bad guys kill people and destroy property, although the movies have their share of those. Some bad guys are just people with no sense of humor and a penchant for disrupting fun. Following is a list of both kinds. Match the characters with the movies in which they appear.

1. Alan Stanwyck
2. Hedley Lamarr
3. Prince Humperdinck
4. Roman Maroni
5. Victor Matlin
6. Vigo the Terrible
7. Ed Rooney
8. Dean Wormer
9. Hans Gruber
10. Murphy Dolan
11. Zod
12. Count De Monet
13. Jafar
14. Tony Montana
15. Mr. Hand
16. Doyle Lonnigan
17. El Guapo
18. Mumbles
19. Clubber Lang
20. Sgt. Hawker

A. *Young Guns*
B. *Johnny Dangerously*
C. *Ghostbusters II*
D. *History of the World Part One*
E. *The Princess Bride*
F. *Animal House*
G. *Fast Times at Ridgemont High*
H. *Fletch*
I. *The Sting*
J. *Blazing Saddles*
K. *Dick Tracy*
L. *Ferris Bueller's Day Off*
M. *Beverly Hills Cop*
N. *Rocky III*
O. *Stripes*
P. *Die Hard*
Q. *Scarface*
R. *Aladdin*
S. *Superman II*
T. *¡Three Amigos!*

1. H
2. J
3. E
4. B
5. M
6. C
7. L
8. F
9. P
10. A

11. S
12. D
13. R
14. Q
15. G
16. I
17. T
18. K
19. N
20. O

Short and Sweet

Sometimes less *is* more, and many of the more memorable movie quotes are but a word or two. You have less to work with here, but all of these one- or two-word quotes should be quite familiar.

1. "They're here."

2. "Here's Johnny!"

3. "Feed me!"

4. "Adrian!"

5. "Yippeekiay, motherfucker."

6. "Shwing!"

7. "Allll-righty then."

8. "Phone home."

9. "Enter!"

10. "Ya folla?"

11. "Meow."

1. Poltergeist
   True or false: This movie was directed by Steven Spielberg?

2. The Shining
   Who directed this film?

3. Little Shop of Horrors
   What is the plant's name in this 1986 movie?

4. Rocky
   Where does Adrian (Talia Shire) work?

5. Die Hard (although this line is in the sequel as well)
   What does MacClane (Bruce Willis) say after he drops the dead terrorist on the police car?

6. Wayne's World
   What business wants to sponsor the show?

7. Ace Ventura, Pet Detective
   What is the name of the Dolphins' mascot?

8. E.T.
   What candy did this alien make popular?

9. The Sunshine Boys
   The Boys reunite to do what sketch?

10. The Sting
    On what horse does Lonnigan (Robert Shaw) bet the half a million dollars?

11. Batman Returns
    What actor plays Max Shrenck?

ANSWERS TO BONUS QUESTIONS

1. False. He cowrote and coproduced, but Tobe Hooper directed.
2. Stanley Kubrick
3. Audrey II
4. in a pet store
5. "Welcome to the party, pal."
6. Noah's Arcade
7. Snowflake
8. Reese's Pieces
9. the doctor sketch
10. Lucky Dan
11. Christopher Walken

12. "Hey, Marvin!"

13. "Carpe diem."

14. "Kmart sucks."

15. "They're back."

12. Midnight Run
    How many times does Jack (Robert De Niro) use this trick on Marvin (John Ashton)?

13. Dead Poets Society
    What does this Latin phrase mean in English?

14. Rain Man
    Where did Raymond's (Dustin Hoffman) father let him drive the car?

15. Poltergeist II
    What actress plays the little girl?

ANSWERS TO BONUS QUESTIONS

12. three
13. Seize the day.

14. in the driveway
15. Heather O'Rourke

Third Time's a Charm

One step past the sequel lies the fine line between a perfect culmination and beating a dead horse. More often than not, Hollywood jumps over this line. But a bad movie does not always mean a lack of good lines. All of the following are from the third in a series.

1. "Like a midget at a urinal, I was gonna have to stay on my toes."

2. "Wouldn't be the Christmas season if the stores were any less hooter than they, hotter than they are . . ."

3. "Keep your distance, but don't look like you're trying to keep your distance. I don't know, fly casual."

4. "I told you, don't call me Junior."

5. "You had the eye of the tiger . . . eye of the tiger, man."

1. Naked Gun 33⅓: The Final Insult
   How does Frank (Leslie Nielsen) say he likes his sex?

2. National Lampoon's Christmas Vacation
   Why is Eddie (Randy Quaid) emptying out his toilet into the sewer?

3. The Return of the Jedi
   Luke (Hamill) tells the Emperor that the Emperor's weakness is his overconfidence. What does the Emperor say Luke's weakness is?

4. Indiana Jones and the Last Crusade
   What are the Jones boys (Harrison Ford and Sean Connery) searching for?

5. Rocky III
   Who plays Thunderlips, the wrestler Rocky fights for charity?

ANSWERS TO BONUS QUESTIONS

1. "I like my sex the way I play basketball—one on one with as little dribbling as possible."
2. "Shitter was full."
3. "Your faith in your friends is yours."
4. the Holy Grail
5. Hulk Hogan

Glad to Have a Friend Like You

Martin and Lewis, Laurel and Hardy, Fred and Ginger. Some unforgettable pairs have, in the history of the movies, delivered some unforgettable lines. Can you name the pair of actors who said the following lines, and in what movies?

1. "Who are those guys?"

2. "We're not worthy. We're not worthy."

3. "That's right, that's right, we bad."

4. "We ain't brothers, we ain't partners, and we ain't friends."

5. "No, I'm chaos and he's mayhem. We're a double act."

6. "We're on a mission from God."

7. "Thank you Mr. Acavano."

1. Paul Newman and Robert Redford in *Butch Cassidy and the Sundance Kid*
2. Mike Myers and Dana Carvey in *Wayne's World*
3. Gene Wilder and Richard Pryor in *Stir Crazy*
4. Eddie Murphy and Nick Nolte in *48 Hours*
5. Mel Gibson and Danny Glover in *Lethal Weapon 3*
6. John Belushi and Dan Aykroyd in *The Blues Brothers*
7. Danny DeVito and Joe Piscopo in *Wise Guys*

Cops and Robbers

One of the oldest formulas around, police chasing bad guys has been an excuse for both comic and dramatic films for ages. More recently, the exchange of bullets has gone hand in hand with the volley of one-liners. Here are a couple of rounds.

1. "We're not gonna fall for a banana in the tailpipe."

2. "I'm too old for this shit."

3. "You look like Marvin Hagler to me. I lost money on Hagler!"

4. "Never stop fighting till the fight is done. . . . Here endeth the lesson."

5. "I didn't kill my wife."
   "I don't care."

6. "I can see this is gonna be a long fuckin' night, convict."

7. "There's no smoking in this building, Ms. Tramell."
   "What are you gonna do? Arrest me for smoking?"

8. "You know, Dick—you mind if I call you Dick?"

1. Beverly Hills Cop
   In trying to cover for Taggert (Ashton) and Rosewood (Judge Reinhold), Foley (Eddie Murphy) tells their boss that they're not "regular" cops. What kind are they?

2. Lethal Weapon
   What character does Joe Pesci play in this film?

3. Red Heat
   What actor plays Ridzik's (Jim Belushi) captain?

4. The Untouchables
   What does Ness (Kevin Costner) say right before the police charge the umbrella warehouse?

5. The Fugitive
   What city is Dr. Kimball (Harrison Ford) from?

6. 48 Hours
   Reggie (Eddie Murphy) asks Jack (Nick Nolte) to tell him a bedtime story. What does Jack say?

7. Basic Instinct
   What is Ms. Tramell's (Sharon Stone) pen name?

8. Dick Tracy
   According to Big Boy (Al Pacino), who said, "A man without a plan is not a man"?

ANSWERS TO BONUS QUESTIONS

1. "They're supercops. And the only thing missing on these guys are capes."
2. Joe Pesci isn't in this movie. He doesn't arrive until the sequel.
3. Peter Boyle
4. "All right, now, let's do some good."
5. Chicago
6. "Jack, tell me a bedtime story."
   "Fuck you."
   "Oh, that's my favorite."
7. Catherine Woolf
8. Nietzsche

9. "Pop quiz, hot shot. There's a bomb on a bus . . . whaddya do?"

10. "Most men your age are getting married and raising up a family. They wouldn't accept prison as a substitute."
    "Sometimes your career's got to come before family."

9. Speed
   What actor plays the villain?

10. Raising Arizona
    According to Glen (Sam McMurray), "Why does it take three Po-
    lacks to screw up a lightbulb?"

ANSWERS TO BONUS QUESTIONS

9. Dennis Hopper

10. " 'Cause they're so darn stupid!"

And the Oscar Goes to . . .

All of the following lines are part of Oscar-winning performances. Can you name the films, the actors, the Oscars they won, and the year the films were released?

1. "I heard that one myself, Bob. Hell, I thought I was dead till I found out it was just that I was in Nebraska."

2. "Oh, you English are so superior, aren't you? Well, would you like to know where you'd be without us, the ole USA, to protect you?"

3. "Well think me a cup of coffee and a chocolate donut with some of those little sprinkles on top, will ya, as long as you're thinking."

4. "Why don't you get yourself a nice girl?"
   "I get a nice one almost every night, Ma."

5. "Do you love him, Loretta?
   "Ma, I love him awful."
   "Oh God, that's too bad."

6. "You better stop eyeballin' me, boy!"

7. "Five fights, huh? Rocky Marciano has got forty and he's a millionaire."

8. "Are you finished?
   "No, I'm just getting warmed up!"

9. "I'm having an old friend for dinner."

10. "Ain't that just like a Wop, brings a knife to a gunfight."

11. "I crap bigger 'n you."

12. "But I didn't cheer . . . They cheated us. This isn't fair. He didn't get out of the cockadoodie car!"

13. "I never kid about money."

14. "Run away when I was twelve years old and I ain't never looked back."
    "Whacha doin' since then?"
    "I run for president . . . I didn't win, though."

15. "That's the thing you gotta remember about WASPs. They love animals, they hate people."

1. Gene Hackman for Best Supporting Actor in *Unforgiven* (1992).
2. Kevin Kline for Best Supporting Actor in *A Fish Called Wanda* (1988).
3. Tommy Lee Jones for Best Supporting Actor in *The Fugitive* (1993).
4. Joe Pesci for Best Supporting Actor in *GoodFellas* (1990).
5. Both Cher and Olympia Dukakis won Oscars for *Moonstruck* (1987). Cher won Best Actress and Dukakis, who played Cher's mother, won Best Supporting Actress.
6. Louis Gossett, Jr., for Best Supporting Actor in *An Officer and a Gentleman* (1982).
7. Jack Nicholson for Best Actor in *One Flew over the Cuckoo's Nest* (1975).
8. Al Pacino for Best Actor in *Scent of a Woman* (1992).
9. Anthony Hopkins for Best Actor in *The Silence of the Lambs* (1991).
10. Sean Connery for Best Supporting Actor in *The Untouchables* (1987).
11. Jack Palance for Best Supporting Actor in *City Slickers* (1991).
12. Kathy Bates for Best Actress in *Misery* (1990).
13. Paul Newman for Best Actor in *The Color of Money* (1986).
14. Denzel Washington for Best Supporting Actor in *Glory* (1989).
15. Michael Douglas for Best Actor in *Wall Street* (1987).

Credits

About Last Night . . . (1986). Screenplay by Tim Kazurinsky & Denise DeClue. Based upon the play *Sexual Perversity in Chicago* by David Mamet.

Ace Ventura, Pet Detective (1994). Screenplay by Jack Bernstein and Tom Shadyac & Jim Carrey. Story by Jack Bernstein.

Airplane! (1980). Written by Jim Abrahams, Jerry Zucker, and David Zucker.

Airplane II: The Sequel (1982). Written by Ken Finkleman.

Aladdin (1992). Written by Ron Clements & John Musker and Ted Elliott & Terry Rossio.

Aliens (1986). Screenplay by James Cameron, Walter Hill, and David Giler. Story by James Cameron and David Giler & Walter Hill, based on characters created by Dan O'Bannon and Ronald Shusett.

American Graffiti (1973). Written by Willard Huyck & Gloria Katz and George Lucas.

. . . And Justice For All (1979). Written by Barry Levinson & Valerie Curtin.

Annie Hall (1977). Written by Woody Allen & Marshall Brickman.

Apocalypse Now (1979). Written by John Milius and Francis Ford Coppola. Narration written by Michael Herr.

Bachelor Party (1984). Screenplay by Neal Israel & Pat Proft. Story by Bob Israel.

Back to School (1986). Screenplay by Steven Kampmann & Will Porter and Peter Torokvei & Harold Ramis. Story by Rodney Dangerfield & Greg Fields & Dennis Snee.

Back to the Future (1985). Written by Robert Zemeckis & Bob Gale.

The Bad News Bears (1976). Written by William Lancaster.

Bananas (1971). Written by Woody Allen & Mickey Rose.

Basic Instinct (1992). Written by Joe Eszterhas.

Batman (1989). Screenplay by Sam Hamm and Warren Skaaren. Story by Sam Hamm. Based upon Batman characters created by Bob Kane and published by DC Comics.

Batman Returns (1992). Screenplay by Daniel Waters. Story by Daniel Waters and Sam Hamm. Based on Batman characters created by Bob Kane and published by DC Comics.

Beetlejuice (1988). Screenplay by Michael McDowell and Warren Skaaren. Story by Michael McDowell & Larry Wilson.

Better Off Dead (1985). Written by Savage Steve Holland.

Beverly Hills Cop (1984). Screenplay by Daniel Petrie, Jr. Story by Danilo Bach and Daniel Petrie, Jr.

Beverly Hills Cop II (1987). Screenplay by Larry Ferguson and Warren Skaaren. Story by Eddie Murphy & Robert D. Wachs. Based on characters created by Danilo Bach and Daniel Petrie, Jr.

Big (1988). Written by Gary Ross & Anne Spielberg.

The Big Chill (1983). Written by Lawrence Kasdan & Barbara Benedek.

Billy Bathgate (1991). Screenplay by Tom Stoppard. Based on the novel by E. L. Doctorow.

Biloxi Blues (1988). Screenplay by Neil Simon. Based on his play.

Blazing Saddles (1973). Screenplay by Mel Brooks, Norman Steinberg, Andrew Bergman, Richard Pryor, and Alan Unger. Story by Andrew Bergman.

The Blues Brothers (1980). Written by Dan Aykroyd & John Landis.

Bob Roberts (1992). Written by Tim Robbins.

Body Heat (1981). Written by Lawrence Kasdan.

The Breakfast Club (1985). Written by John Hughes.

Brighton Beach Memoirs (1986). Screenplay by Neil Simon. Based on his play.

Broadcast News (1987). Written by James L. Brooks.

A Bronx Tale (1993). Screenplay by Chazz Palminteri. Based on his play.

Bugsy (1991). Written by James Toback. Based on research drawn from the book *We Only Kill Each Other: The Life and Bad Times of Bugsy Siegel* by Dean Jennings.

Bull Durham (1988). Written by Ron Sheldon.

Butch Cassidy and the Sundance Kid (1969). Written by William Goldman.

Caddyshack (1980). Written by Brian Doyle-Murray & Harold Ramis & Douglas Kenney.

Cape Fear (1991). Screenplay by Wesley Strick. Based on screenplay by James R. Webb and the novel *The Executioners* by John D. MacDonald.

Casual Sex? (1988). Screenplay by Wendy Goldman & Judy Toll.

City Slickers (1991). Written by Lowell Ganz & Babaloo Mandel.

City Slickers II: The Legend of Curly's Gold (1994). Written by Billy Crystal & Lowell Ganz & Babaloo Mandel. Based on characters created by Lowell Ganz & Babaloo Mandel.

Close Encounters of the Third Kind (1977). Written by Steven Spielberg.

Club Paradise (1986). Screenplay by Brian Doyle-Murray & Harold Ramis. Story by Ed Roboto & Tom Leopold and Chris Miller & David Standish.

Cocktail (1988). Screenplay by Heywood Gould. Based on his novel.

Cocoon (1985). Screenplay by Tom Benedek. Based on characters created by David Saperstein.

The Color of Money (1986). Screenplay by Richard Price. Based on the novel by Walter Tevis.

Coming to America (1988). Screenplay by David Sheffield & Barry W. Blaustein. Story by Eddie Murphy.

Commando (1985). Screenplay by Steven E. de Souza. Story by Joseph Loeb III & Matthew Weisman and Steven E. de Souza.

The Commitments (1991). Screenplay by Dick Clement & Ian La Frenais and Roddy Doyle. From the novel by Roddy Doyle.

Cool Hand Luke (1967). Screenplay by Donn Pearce and Frank R. Pierson. Based on the novel by Donn Pearce.

Crimes and Misdemeanors (1989). Written by Woody Allen.

Crocodile Dundee (1986). Screenplay by Paul Hogan, Ken Shadie, and John Cornell. Story by Paul Hogan.

Dead Again (1991). Written by Scott Frank.

Dead Poets Society (1989). Written by Tom Schulman.

Death Becomes Her (1992). Written by Martin Donovan & David Koepp.

Deliverance (1972). Screenplay by James Dickey. Based on his novel.

Dick Tracy (1990). Written by Jim Cash & Jack Epps, Jr. Based on characters created by Chester Gould for the "Dick Tracy" comic strip.

Die Hard (1988). Screenplay by Jeb Stuart and Steven E. de Souza. Based on the novel *Nothing Lasts Forever* by Roderick Thorp.

Die Hard 2 (1990). Screenplay by Steven E. de Souza and Doug Richardson. Based on the novel *58 Minutes* by Walter Wager.

Diner (1982). Written by Barry Levinson.

Dirty Harry (1971). Screenplay by Harry Julian Fink & R. M. Fink and Dean Riesner. Story by Harry Julian Fink & R. M. Fink.

Dirty Rotten Scoundrels (1988). Screenplay by Dale Launer and Stanley Shapiro & Paul Henning.

Do the Right Thing (1989). Written by Spike Lee.

Dragnet (1987). Written by Dan Aykroyd, Alan Zweibel, and Tom Mankiewicz.

Eight Men Out (1988). Screenplay by John Sayles. Based on the book *Eight Men Out* by Eliot Asinof.

The Elephant Man (1980). Screenplay by Christopher de Vore & Eric Bergren & David Lynch. Based on books entitled *The Elephant Man* by Sir Frederick Treves and Ashley Montagu.

The Empire Strikes Back (1980). Screenplay by Lawrence Kasdan and Leigh Brackett. Story by George Lucas.

E.T. (1982). Written by Melissa Mathison.

Everything You Always Wanted to Know about Sex (but were afraid to ask) (1972). Screenplay by Woody Allen.

Excalibur (1981). Story by Rospo Pallenberg and John Boorman. Adapted from Thomas Malory's *Le Morte d'Arthur* by Rospo Pallenberg.

The Exorcist (1973). Story by William Peter Blatty. Based on his novel.

Falling Down (1993). Written by Ebbe Roe Smith.

Fast Times at Ridgemont High (1982). Screenplay by Cameron Crowe.

Fatal Attraction (1987). Screenplay by James Dearden.

Ferris Bueller's Day Off (1986). Written by John Hughes.

A Few Good Men (1992). Screenplay by Aaron Sorkin. Based on his play.

Field of Dreams (1989). Screenplay by Phil Alden Robinson. Based on the book *Shoeless Joe* by W. P. Kinsella.

A Fish Called Wanda (1988). Screenplay by John Cleese and Charles Crichton.

The Flamingo Kid (1984). Screenplay by Neal Marshall & Garry K. Marshall. Story by Neal Marshall.

Fletch (1985). Screenplay by Andrew Bergman. Based on the novel by Gregory McDonald.

Fletch Lives (1989). Written by Leon Capetanos. Based on characters created by Gregory McDonald.

The Fly (1986). Screenplay by Charles Edward Pogue and David Cronenberg. From the story by George Langelaan.

48 Hours (1982). Written by Roger Spottiswoode, Walter Hill, Larry Gross, and Steven E. de Souza.

Foul Play (1978). Written by Colin Higgins.

Fraternity Vacation (1985). Written by Lindsay Harrison.

The Freshman (1990). Written by Andrew Bergman.

The Fugitive (1993). Screenplay by Jeb Stuart and David Twohy. Story by David Twohy. Based on characters created by Roy Huggins.

Ghostbusters (1984). Written by Dan Aykroyd and Harold Ramis.

Ghostbusters II (1989). Written by Harold Ramis and Dan Aykroyd. Based on characters created by Dan Aykroyd and Harold Ramis.

Glengarry Glen Ross (1992). Screenplay by David Mamet. Based on his play.

Glory (1989). Screenplay by Kevin Jarre. Based on the books *Lay This Laurel* by Lincoln Kirstein and *One Gallant Rush* by Peter Burchard and the letters of Robert Gould Shaw.

The Godfather (1972). Screenplay by Mario Puzo and Francis Ford Coppola. Based on the novel by Mario Puzo.

The Godfather Part II (1974). Screenplay by Francis Ford Coppola and Mario Puzo. Based on the novel by Mario Puzo.

The Godfather Part III (1990). Written by Mario Puzo and Francis Ford Coppola.

GoodFellas (1990). Screenplay by Nicholas Pileggi & Martin Scorsese. Based on the book *Wiseguy* by Nicholas Pileggi.

Good Morning, Vietnam (1987). Written by Mitch Markowitz.

The Graduate (1967). Screenplay by Calder Willingham and Buck Henry. Based on the novel by Charles Webb.

Grease (1978). Screenplay by Bronte Woodard. Adaptation by Allan Carr. Based on the musical by Jim Jacobs & Warren Casey.

Groundhog Day (1993). Screenplay by Danny Rubin and Harold Ramis. Story by Danny Rubin.

Hannah and Her Sisters (1986). Written by Woody Allen.

Heathers (1988). Written by Daniel Waters.

High Anxiety (1977). Written by Mel Brooks, Ronald Clark, Rudy DeLuca, and Barry Levinson.

History of the World Part One (1981). Written by Mel Brooks.

Hollywood Shuffle (1987). Written by Robert Townsend & Keenen Ivory Wayans.

Honeymoon in Vegas (1992). Written by Andrew Bergman.

Hoosiers (1986). Written by Angelo Pizzo.

Hot Shots! (1991). Written by Jim Abrahams & Pat Proft.

Hot Shots! Part Deux (1993). Written by Jim Abrahams & Pat Proft. Based on characters created by Jim Abrahams and Pat Proft.

The Hunt for Red October (1990). Screenplay by Larry Ferguson and Donald Stewart. Based on the novel by Tom Clancy.

I'm Gonna Git You Sucka (1988). Written by Keenen Ivory Wayans.

Indecent Proposal (1993). Screenplay by Amy Holden Jones. Based on the novel by Jack Engelhard.

Indiana Jones and the Last Crusade (1989). Story by George Lucas and Menno Meyjes. Based on characters created by George Lucas and Philip Kaufman. Screenplay by Jeffrey Boam.

Indiana Jones and the Temple of Doom (1984). Screenplay by Willard Huyck & Gloria Katz. Story by George Lucas.

The In-Laws (1979). Written by Andrew Bergman.

In the Line of Fire (1993). Written by Jeff Maguire.

Jaws (1975). Screenplay by Carl Gottlieb and Peter Benchley. Based on the novel by Peter Benchley.

Jaws 2 (1978). Written by Carl Gottlieb and Howard Sackler.

The Jerk (1979). Screenplay by Michael Elias and Steve Martin & Carl Gottlieb. Story by Steve Martin and Carl Gottlieb.

JFK (1991). Screenplay by Oliver Stone & Zachary Sklar. Based on the books *Trail of the Assassins* by Jim Garrison and *Crossfire: The Plot That Killed Kennedy* by Jim Marrs.

Johnny Dangerously (1984). Written by Norman Steinberg, Jeff Harris, Bernie Kukoff, and Harry Colomby.

The Karate Kid (1984). Written by Robert Mark Kamen.

The Kentucky Fried Movie (1977). Written by Jim Abrahams, Jerry Zucker, and David Zucker.

Kindergarten Cop (1990). Screenplay by Murray Salem and Herschel Weingrod & Timothy Harris. Story by Murray Salem.

L.A. Story (1991). Written by Steve Martin.

A League of Their Own (1992). Screenplay by Lowell Ganz & Babaloo Mandel. Based on the story by Kim Wilson & Kelly Candaele.

Lean on Me (1989). Written by Michael Schiffer.

Lethal Weapon (1987). Written by Shane Black.

Lethal Weapon 2 (1989). Screenplay by Jeffrey Boam. Story by Shane Black & Warren Murphy. Based on characters created by Shane Black.

Lethal Weapon 3 (1992). Screenplay by Jeffrey Boam and Robert Mark Kamen. Story by Jeffrey Boam. Based on characters created by Shane Black.

Little Shop of Horrors (1986). Screenplay by Howard Ashman. Based on musical play which was based on film by Roger Corman.

Lost in America (1985). Written by Albert Brooks & Monica Johnson.

Love and Death (1975). Written by Woody Allen.

Major League (1989). Written by David S. Ward.

Major League II (1994). Screenplay by R. J. Stewart. Story by R. J. Stewart and Tom S. Parker & Jim Jennewein. Based on characters created by David S. Ward.

Malcolm X (1992). Screenplay by Arnold Perl and Spike Lee. Based on the book *The Autobiography of Malcolm X* by Alex Haley and Malcolm X.

The Man with Two Brains (1983). Written by George Gipe, Steve Martin, and Carl Reiner.

Marathon Man (1976). Screenplay by William Goldman. Based on his novel.

Meatballs (1979). Written by Harold Ramis, Len Blum, Dan Goldberg, and Janis Allen.

Midnight Cowboy (1969). Screenplay by Waldo Salt. Based on the novel by James Leo Herlihy.

Midnight Run (1988). Written by George Gallo.

Misery (1990). Screenplay by William Goldman. Based on the novel by Stephen King.

Mississippi Burning (1988). Written by Chris Gerolmo.

Mr. Saturday Night (1992). Written by Billy Crystal and Lowell Ganz & Babaloo Mandel.

Mo' Better Blues (1990). Written by Spike Lee.

Monty Python and the Holy Grail (1975). Written by Graham Chapman, John Cleese, Terry Gilliam, Eric Idle, and Michael Palin.

Monty Python's Life of Brian (1979). Written by Graham Chapman, John Cleese, Terry Gilliam, Eric Idle, Terry Jones, and Michael Palin.

Monty Python's The Meaning of Life (1983). Written by Graham Chapman, John Cleese, Terry Gilliam, Eric Idle, Terry Jones, and Michael Palin.

Moonstruck (1987). Written by John Patrick Shanley.

Murder by Death (1976). Written by Neil Simon.

My Cousin Vinny (1992). Written by Dale Launer.

My Favorite Year (1982). Screenplay by Norman Steinberg and Dennis Palumbo. Story by Dennis Palumbo.

The Naked Gun: From the Files of Police Squad! (1988). Written by Jerry Zucker & Jim Abrahams & David Zucker & Pat Proft. Based on the TV series *Police Squad* created by Jim Abrahams & David Zucker & Jerry Zucker.

The Naked Gun 2½: The Smell of Fear (1991). Written by David Zucker & Pat Proft. Based on the TV series *Police Squad* created by Jim Abrahams & David Zucker & Jerry Zucker.

The Naked Gun 33⅓: The Final Insult (1994). Written by Pat Proft and David Zucker & Robert Lo Cash. Based on the TV series *Police Squad* created by Jim Abrahams & David Zucker & Jerry Zucker.

National Lampoon's Animal House (1978). Written by Chris Miller & Harold Ramis & Douglas Kenney.

National Lampoon's Christmas Vacation (1989). Written by John Hughes.

National Lampoon's European Vacation (1985). Screenplay by John Hughes and Robert Klane. Story by John Hughes.

National Lampoon's Vacation (1983). Screenplay by John Hughes. Based on his magazine article.

The Natural (1984). Screenplay by Roger Towne and Phil Dusenberry. Based on the novel by Bernard Malamud.

Night Shift (1982). Written by Lowell Ganz & Babaloo Mandel.

Nothing in Common (1986). Written by Rick Podell & Michael Preminger.

An Officer and a Gentleman (1982). Written by Douglas Day Stewart.

One Flew over the Cuckoo's Nest (1975). Screenplay by Bo Goldman and Lawrence Hauben. Based on the novel by Ken Kesey.

The Outsiders (1983). Screenplay by Kathleen Knutsen Rowell. Based on the novel by S. E. Hinton.

Peggy Sue Got Married (1986). Story by Jerry Leichtling & Arlene Sarner.

The Pink Panther Strikes Again (1976). Written by Frank Waldman & Blake Edwards.

Planes, Trains and Automobiles (1987). Written by John Hughes.

The Player (1992). Screenplay by Michael Tolkin. Based on his novel.

Police Academy 2: Their First Assignment (1985). Written by Barry Blaustein & David Sheffield. Based on characters created by Neil Israel & Pat Proft.

Poltergeist (1982). Screenplay by Michael Grais & Mark Victor and Steven Spielberg. Story by Steven Spielberg.

Poltergeist II (1986). Written by Michael Grais and Mark A. Victor. Based on characters created by Steven Spielberg.

Porky's (1982). Written by Bob Clark.

Predator (1987). Written by Jim Thomas & John Thomas.

Pretty Woman (1990). Written by J. F. Lawton.

The Princess Bride (1987). Screenplay by William Goldman. Based on his novel.

Prizzi's Honor (1985). Screenplay by Richard Condon and Janet Roach. Based on the novel by Richard Condon.

The Producers (1968). Written by Mel Brooks.

Quick Change (1990). Screenplay by Howard Franklin. Based on the book by Jay Cronley.

Raging Bull (1980). Screenplay by Mardik Martin and Paul Schrader. Based on the autobiography by Jake La Motta.

Raiders of the Lost Ark (1981). Screenplay by Lawrence Kasdan. Story by George Lucas and Philip Kaufman.

Rain Man (1988). Screenplay by Ronald Bass and Barry Morrow. Story by Barry Morrow.

Raising Arizona (1987). Written by Ethan & Joel Coen.

Real Genius (1985). Screenplay by Neal Israel & Pat Proft and Peter Torokvei. Story by Neal Israel and Pat Proft.

Red Heat (1988). Screenplay by Harry Kleiner & Walter Hill and Troy Kennedy Martin. Story by Walter Hill.

Repo Man (1984). Written by Alex Cox.

Reservoir Dogs (1992). Written by Quentin Tarantino.

Return of the Jedi (1983). Screenplay by George Lucas and Lawrence Kasdan. Story by George Lucas.

The Return of the Pink Panther (1975). Written by Blake Edwards & Frank Waldman.

Revenge of the Nerds (1984). Screenplay by Steve Zacharias & Jeff Buhai. Story by Steve Zacharias & Jeff Buhai and Tim Metcalfe & Miguel Tejada-Flores.

Risky Business (1983). Written by Paul Brickman.

Road House (1989). Screenplay by David Lee Henry and Hilary Henkin. Story by David Lee Henry.

Robin Hood: Prince of Thieves (1991). Screenplay by Pen Densham & John Watson. Story by Pen Densham.

Robocop (1987). Written by Edward Neumeier & Michael Miner.

Rocky (1976). Written by Sylvester Stallone.

Rocky II (1979). Written by Sylvester Stallone.

Rocky III (1982). Written by Sylvester Stallone.

Rocky IV (1985). Written by Sylvester Stallone.

Romancing the Stone (1984). Written by Diane Thomas.

Roxanne (1987). Screenplay by Steve Martin. Based on the play *Cyrano de Bergerac* by Edmond Rostand.

The Running Man (1987). Screenplay by Steven E. de Souza. Based on the novel by Richard Bachman.

Running Scared (1986). Screenplay by Gary Devore and Jimmy Huston. Story by Gary Devore.

Ruthless People (1986). Written by Dane Launer.

St. Elmo's Fire (1985). Written by Carl Kurlander & Joel Schumacher.

Saturday Night Fever (1977). Screenplay by Norman Wexler. Based on a story by Nik Cohn.

Say Anything . . . (1989). Written by Cameron Crowe.

Scarface (1983). Screenplay by Oliver Stone. Based on the book by Armitage Trail.

Scent of a Woman (1992). Screenplay by Bo Goldman. Suggested by a character from "Profumo Di Donna" by Ruggero Maccari and Dino Risi based on the novel *Il Buio E Il Miele* by Giovanni Arpino.

Scrooged (1988). Written by Mitch Glazer and Michael O'Donoghue. Suggested by *A Christmas Carol* by Charles Dickens.

The Secret of My Success (1987). Screenplay by Jim Cash & Jack Epps, Jr. and A. J. Carothers. Story by A. J. Carothers.

Seems Like Old Times (1980). Written by Neil Simon.

She's Gotta Have It (1986). Written by Spike Lee.

The Shining (1979). Screenplay by Stanley Kubrick & Diane Johnson. Based on the novel by Stephen King.

Short Circuit (1986). Written by S. S. Wilson & Brent Maddock.

The Silence of the Lambs (1991). Screenplay by Ted Tally. Based on the novel by Thomas Harris.

Silent Movie (1976). Screenplay by Mel Brooks, Ron Clark, Rudy de Luca, and Barry Levinson. Story by Ron Clark.

Singles (1992). Written by Cameron Crowe.

Sixteen Candles (1984). Written by John Hughes.

Slap Shot (1977). Written by Nancy Dowd.

Sleeper (1973). Written by Woody Allen & Marshall Brickman.

Smokey and the Bandit (1977). Screenplay by Charles Shyer & Alan Mandel and James Lee Barrett. Story by Hal Needham & Robert L. Levy.

Soapdish (1991). Screenplay by Robert Harling and Andrew Bergman. Story by Robert Harling.

Something Wild (1986). Written by E. Max Frye.

Spaceballs (1987). Written by Mel Brooks & Thomas Meehan & Ronny Graham.

Speed (1994). Written by Graham Yost.

Spies Like Us (1985). Screenplay by Dan Aykroyd and Lowell Ganz & Babaloo Mandel. Story by Dan Aykroyd & David Thomas.

Splash (1984). Screenplay by Lowell Ganz & Babaloo Mandel and Bruce Jay Friedman. Screen story by Bruce Jay Friedman. Based on a story by Brian Grazer.

Stakeout (1987). Written by Jim Kouf.

Star Wars (1977). Written by George Lucas.

The Sting (1973). Written by David S. Ward.

Stir Crazy (1980). Written by Bruce Jay Friedman.

Stripes (1981). Written by Harold Ramis & Len Blum & Dan Goldberg.

Sudden Impact (1983). Screenplay by Joseph C. Stinson. Story by Earl E. Smith & Charles B. Pierce.

The Sunshine Boys (1975). Screenplay by Neil Simon. Based on his play.

Superman (1978). Screenplay by Mario Puzo and Robert Benton and David Newman & Leslie Newman.

Superman 2 (1980). Screenplay by Mario Puzo and David Newman & Leslie Newman. Story by Mario Puzo.

The Sure Thing (1985). Written by Steven L. Bloom and Jonathan Roberts.

Take the Money and Run (1969). Screenplay by Woody Allen & Mickey Rose.

Taxi Driver (1976). Written by Paul Schrader.

Tequila Sunrise (1988). Written by Robert Towne.

The Terminator (1984). Written by James Cameron & Gale Ann Hurd.

Terminator 2: Judgment Day (1991). Written by James Cameron and William Wisher.

This Is Spinal Tap (1984). Written by Christopher Guest & Michael McKean & Rob Reiner & Harry Shearer.

¡Three Amigos! (1986). Written by Steve Martin & Lorne Michaels & Randy Newman.

Throw Momma from the Train (1987). Written by Stu Silver.

Tin Men (1987). Written by Barry Levinson.

Tombstone (1993). Written by Kevin Jarre.

Tootsie (1982). Screenplay by Murray Schisgal and Larry Gelbart. Story by Larry Gelbart and Don McGuire.

Top Gun (1986). Written by Jim Cash & Jack Epps, Jr.

Top Secret! (1984). Written by Jim Abrahams & Jerry Zucker & David Zucker and Martyn Burke.

Total Recall (1990). Screenplay by Ronald Shushett & Dan O'Bannon and Gary Goldman. Screen story by Ronald Shushett & Dan O'Bannon and Jon Povill. Inspired by the short story "We Can Remember It for You Wholesale" by Philip K. Dick.

Trading Places (1983). Written by Timothy Harris & Herschel Weingrod.

Twins (1988). Written by William Davies & William Osborne and Timothy Harris & Herschel Weingrod.

Uncle Buck (1989). Written by John Hughes.

Unforgiven (1992). Written by David Webb Peoples.

The Untouchables (1987). Written by David Mamet. Suggested by the TV series and based on the works written by Oscar Fraley with Eliot Ness and with Paul Robsky.

Wall Street (1987). Written by Stanley Weiser & Oliver Stone.

The Wanderers (1979). Screenplay by Philip & Rose Kaufman. Based on the novel by Richard Price.

WarGames (1983). Written by Lawrence Lasker & Walter F. Parkes.

Wayne's World (1992). Written by Mike Myers and Bonnie Turner & Terry Turner. Based on characters created by Mike Myers.

Weekend at Bernie's (1989). Written by Robert Klane.

What about Bob? (1991). Screenplay by Tom Schulman. Story by Alvin Sargent & Laura Ziskin.

When Harry Met Sally . . . (1989). Written by Nora Ephron.

White Men Can't Jump (1992). Written by Ron Shelton.

Who Framed Roger Rabbit (1988). Screenplay by Jeffrey Price & Peter S. Seaman. Based on the book *Who Censored Roger Rabbit?* by Gary K. Wold.

Who's Harry Crumb? (1989). Story by Robert Conte & Peter Martin Wortmann.

Wise Guys (1986). Written by George Gallo.

The Witches of Eastwick (1987). Screenplay by Michael Cristofer. Based on the novel by John Updike.

Working Girl (1988). Written by Kevin Wade.

Young Frankenstein (1974). Screen story and screenplay by Gene Wilder & Mel Brooks. Based on characters in the novel *Frankenstein* by Mary Wollenstonecraft Shelley.

Young Guns (1988). Written by John Fusco.

Young Guns II (1990). Written by John Fusco. Based on characters created by John Fusco.

Index of Movies

Page references are to lines of dialogue.